Glencoe Science

LAB MANUAL

Probeware
for Biology

science.glencoe.com

Glencoe

New York, New York   Columbus, Ohio   Chicago, Illinois   Peoria, Illinois   Woodland Hills, California

Credits

Each *Probeware Lab Manual for Biology* activity was reviewed by Vernier Software & Technology.

 **Glencoe**

The McGraw·Hill Companies

Send all inquiries to:
Glencoe/McGraw-Hill
8787 Orion Place
Columbus, OH 43240-4027

ISBN 0-07-860225-4

Printed in the United States of America.

10 11 REL 11 10 09

Contents

To the Teacher

What are Probeware Labs?

This *Probeware Lab Manual for Biology* contains 10 probeware laboratory activities that are designed for a high school biology curriculum. Each activity helps students explore scientific concepts using a probeware data collection system. These hand-held systems provide a fast and simple way to collect, view, and analyze data in the classroom or during a field investigation. Using various probes and sensors, students can measure temperature, light, voltage, conductivity, motion, pH, and more. Integrating technology in the classroom is made simple with step-by-step instructions for setting up and using the probeware.

What are the components of a probeware system?

- **CBL 2™ or LabPro® data collection unit** collects data from the probes and sends it to the graphing calculator.
- **DataMate** is a software program that is used to collect and plot data. DataMate comes loaded on the CBL 2 or LabPro unit and is transferred to the graphing calculator for use.
- **TI-73 or TI-83 Plus Graphing Calculator** displays and analyzes data. The activities in the manual were written for use with a TI-73 or TI-83 Plus graphing calculator although several other TI graphing calculators are compatible with both data collection units.
- **Probes** collect data. A wide variety of probes are available for the CBL 2 and LabPro systems. A list of the specific probes needed for this book is found on page 8.

What does the Teacher Guide provide?

- **Objectives** gives a brief description of the purpose of each activity.
- **Process Skills** lists scientific skills students will be practicing (i.e. form hypotheses, experiment, interpret data, measure, predict).
- **Time Allotment** provides approximate time requirements for each activity.
- **Materials** provides additional information about the supplies needed in the activity (i.e. amount or number of materials needed or alternate materials).
- **Preparation** includes instructions on how to prepare activity materials and equipment before the activity begins.
- **Teaching the Lab** provides background knowledge students may need and concepts that should be reviewed before performing the activity. Suggestions for size of student groups appropriate for the activity are provided.
- **Analysis** provides correct responses to the student lab questions. These questions are designed to encourage thought and discussion about important concepts needed to successfully comprehend the activity. Discuss the answers with students to ensure their understanding of the processes and concepts presented during the lab.

This Teacher Edition also supplies information designed to give you as much help as possible in preparing for each activity.

Correlation to Glencoe Biology Programs

The activities in the *Probeware Lab Manual for Biology* coordinate with the following chapters/units in these Glencoe biology programs. Use this chart to help plan the best way to use these activities with your class.

HS Probeware for Biolog Lab Manual: Correlation Chart   2/3/06

	Glencoe Biology	Biology: The Dynamics of Life	BSCS Biology: A Molecular Approach	Biology: An Everyday Experience	Biology: Living Systems
Is oxygen cycled in the environment?	Chapter 2	Chapters 2, 9	Chapters 24	Chapters 31	——————
An Environmental Limiting Factor	Chapter 2	Chapters 3, 6	Chapters 24	Chapters 31	Chapters 28
Testing Water Quality	Chapters 3, 5	Chapter 5	Chapter 25	Chapter 32	Chapter 30
How well does yeast ferment different sugars?	Chapter 8	Chapter 9	Chapter 5	——————	Chapter 6
How can pH be used to compare rates of photosynthesis?	Chapter8	Chapter 21	Chapter 4	Chapter 6,19	Chapter 6
Effect of Environmental Temperature on the Metabolic Rates of Animals	Chapter 35	Chapters 30, 31	Chapter 2	Chapters 14, 12,13,15	Chapter 28
What is the effect of exercise on body temperature?	Chapter 34	Chapter 34	Chapters 5	Chapter 11	Chapter 28
Measuring Response Time	Chapter 33	Chapter 36	Chapter 21	Chapter 15	Chapter 25
Breathing and Heart Rate	Chapter 34	Chapter 37	Chapters 7	Chapters 11	Chapter 21
What is the effect of exercise on heart rate?	Chapter 34	Chapter 37	Chapter 7	Chapter 11	Chapter 21

Safety and Disposal of Lab Materials

Teaching science requires the use of certain supplies and safety equipment to maintain a safe classroom. The activities in the *Glencoe Science Probeware Lab Manual for Biology* minimize dangers in the laboratory. Even so, there are no guarantees against accidents. For additional help, refer to the booklet *Glencoe Laboratory Management and Safety in the Science Classroom,* which contains safety guidelines and masters to test students' lab and safety skills.

General Guidelines

- Post safety guidelines, fire escape routes, and a list of emergency procedures in the classroom. Make sure students understand these procedures. Remind them at the beginning of *every* lab session.
- Understand and make note of the Safety Symbols used in the activities.
- Have students fill out a safety contract. Students should pledge to follow the rules, to wear safety attire, and to conduct themselves in a responsible manner.
- Know where emergency equipment is stored and how to use it.
- Perform all activities before you allow students to do so.
- Supervise students at all times. Check assembly of all setups.
- Instruct students to follow directions carefully and to not take shortcuts or switch steps.
- Make sure that all students are wearing proper safety attire. Do not permit wearing contact lenses, even with safety glasses; splashing chemicals could infuse under a lens and cause eye damage.

Handling Electronic Equipment

- Instruct students on the safety guidelines provided by the manufacturer of your calculator(s) and probe(s).
- Check wiring for damage before each use. Do not use if frayed.
- Do not use the equipment where it could get wet.
- Do not allow students to eat or drink while using the equipment.
- Unplug the calculator when not in use.

- Caution students to use care when handling the equipment. Calculators and probes should not be shaken or dropped.
- Store the equipment properly when not in use.

Handling Chemicals

- Always wear safety goggles, gloves, and an apron when handling chemicals. Treat all chemicals as potentially dangerous.
- Never ingest chemicals. Use proper techniques to smell solutions.
- Use a fume hood when handling chemicals that are poisonous or corrosive or that give off a vapor.
- Know the location of an eyewash station. Flush the eyewash for five minutes once a week to remove harmful contaminants that may grow in the eyewash. Do not use a squeeze bottle as a substitute for an eyewash.
- Always add acids to water, never the reverse.
- Prepare solutions by adding the solid to a small amount of distilled water and then diluting with water to the volume listed. If you use a hydrate that is different from the one specified in a particular preparation, you will need to adjust the amount of hydrate to obtain the correct concentration.
- Consider purchasing premixed solutions from a scientific supply house to reduce the amount of chemicals on hand.
- Maintain appropriate MSDS (Materials Safety Data Sheets) in the laboratory.

Chemical Storage

- Use wood shelving, rather than metal, that is firmly attached to the wall.
- Equip shelves with a lip to prevent chemicals from being jarred off the shelf.

- Store only those chemicals you intend to use.
- Store chemicals in upright positions no more than three containers deep.
- Store chemicals at or below eye level but not on the floor.
- Make sure all containers are labeled to identify the contents, concentration, date purchased or prepared, safety precautions for handling, expiration date, and manufacturer's name and address.
- Separate chemicals by reaction type. For example, store acids in one place and bases in another. Store oxidants away from easily oxidized materials.
- Store flammables in an approved flammable cabinet.

Chemical Disposal

- Maintain an ongoing chemical inventory. Remove chemicals that are out-of-date, contaminated, or lacking legible labels.
- Consult local and state authorities for disposal methods. Use a reference such as *Prudent Practices in the Laboratory: Handling and Disposal of Chemicals* (National Academy Press, 1995) for general guidelines on handling and disposing of chemicals. Current laws in your area supersede the information in this book.
- Neutralize any substance that has a pH less than 3 or greater than 8 before disposal.

- For substances that can be flushed down a drain, flush with at least 100 times its volume of tap water.
- Consider utilizing a commercial chemical disposal company.

Chemical Spills

- Maintain a clearly identified spill kit in the science lab that contains commercial materials for that purpose. You also can keep a container of dry sand or dry clay available; remember that these will not neutralize an acid or base.
- Contain the spill and neutralize the chemical if necessary.
- Remove the material with equipment made of plastic or polypropylene to prevent reaction with any chemical that remains.
- Place the material in plastic bags or containers and label appropriately.
- Inform the custodial staff of proper disposal of the material.
- For a major spill, such as breaking a liter bottle of hydrochloric acid, take the following actions:
  ➤ Evacuate all students through the exits farthest from the spill.
  ➤ Assist any person splashed with the chemical to the safety shower.
  ➤ Contain the spill wearing proper protective clothing. Do not allow the spill to trap you.
  ➤ Call for help.

DISCLAIMER

Glencoe/McGraw-Hill makes no claims to the completeness of this discussion of laboratory safety and chemical storage. The information presented is not all-inclusive, nor does it address all of the hazards associated with the handling, storage, and disposal of chemicals, or with laboratory practices and management.

Materials

It is assumed that goggles, laboratory aprons, tap water, distilled water, textbooks, paper, calculators, pencils, pens, weighing paper or dishes, and balances are available for all activities. The quantities listed in the Teacher Guide pages are needed for each individual or group performing the activity.

Probeware Equipment	Lab 1	Lab 2	Lab 3	Lab 4	Lab 5	Lab 6	Lab 7	Lab 8	Lab 9	Lab 10
AC adapters	X		X	X	X					
Carbon dioxide sensor				X		X				
C-clamp								X		
CBL 2 or LabPro interface	X									
CBL 2 or LabPro unit	X	X	X	X	X	X	X	X	X	X
Light-intensity sensor										
Link cable	X	X	X	X	X	X	X	X	X	X
Motion detector (sensor)								X		
pH sensor		X			X					
Respiration chamber (comes with CO_2 sensor)						X				
Temperature probe				X			X			
Texas Instruments graphing calculator	X	X	X	X	X	X	X	X	X	X
Vernier dissolved oxygen probe	X		X							
Vernier Exercise Heart Rate Monitor									X	X

Biological	Lab 1	Lab 2	Lab 3	Lab 4	Lab 5	Lab 6	Lab 7	Lab 8	Lab 9	Lab 10
Aquatic animal, such as a snail	X									
Aquatic plant, such as Elodea	X				X					
Soil samples		X								
Terrestrial animal, such as a cricket						X				

Chemical	Lab 1	Lab 2	Lab 3	Lab 4	Lab 5	Lab 6	Lab 7	Lab 8	Lab 9	Lab 10
D.O. electrode filling solution (KCl solution)	X		X							
Sodium sulfite calibration solution (included with probes)			X							
Sugar solutions—examples (12mL each): glucose, sucrose, fructose, dextrose, maltose, lactose				X						
Water, dechlorinated					X					
Water, distilled	X	X	X		X					
Water, tap (allowed to stand for one day)	X					X				
Water, hot and cold				X						
Water samples			X							
drinking water		X								
ocean/saltwater aquarium		X								
precipitation		X								
various bodies of water		X								
Yeast suspension, 12 mL per 12 mL of sugar solution				X						

Laboratory Equipment	Lab 1	Lab 2	Lab 3	Lab 4	Lab 5	Lab 6	Lab 7	Lab 8	Lab 9	Lab 10
Balance		X				X				
Barometer			X							
Beaker, 150-mL										
250-mL	X	X	X		X					
500-mL						X				
1000-mL						X				
Beral pipette	X		X			X				
Chairs									X	
Containers, small clear, with caps, to be used for the closed systems	X									
Dissolved oxygen calibration bottles (included with probes)	X		X							
Exercise equipment										X
Gloves, plastic or rubber		X	X		X					
Goggles	X	X	X	X	X	X	X		X	X
Graduated cylinder, 10-mL	X		X	X						
100-mL	X		X							
Jars with lids		X	X	X						
Laboratory aprons	X	X	X	X	X	X	X		X	X
Light source, artificial, various	X				X					
Mortar and pestle		X								
Rinse bottles					X					
Ruler, metric	X		X							
Spoon, large		X								
Stirring rods				X						
Stopwatch				X					X	X
Test tube, large				X	X					
Test-tube rack					X					
Test-tube stoppers					X					
Thermal mitts (pairs)				X						
Thermometer, Celsius				X						
classroom model			X							
Water bath				X						

Consumables	Lab 1	Lab 2	Lab 3	Lab 4	Lab 5	Lab 6	Lab 7	Lab 8	Lab 9	Lab 10
Athletic tape							X			
Colored pencils									X	
Lab wipes	X		X							
Paper plates		X								
Paper towels						X				
Plastic bags		X					X			
Polyester fill or wool insulate temp. probe							X			
Wax marking pencil	X	X	X							

Preparation of Solutions

Solutions used in the laboratory manual are listed in order by the number of the activity in which they are used. Preparation procedures, cautions, and amounts to make are also included. You may want to plan several weeks ahead so you will have all the solutions prepared.

Lab	Solution	Preparation	Cautions
Lab 3	2.0 M sodium sulfite solution	Add 25 g solid anhydrous sodium sulfite crystals (Na_2SO_3) to enough distilled water to make 100 mL of solution. Prepare the solution 24 hours in advance of calibrating the dissolved oxygen probe to ensure all oxygen has been depleted.	Possible tissue irritant. Moderately toxic in solid form. Avoid contact with skin and eyes. Flush with water if body contact occurs.
Lab 4	Sugar solutions	5% sugar solution: add 5 g sugar to a container and add enough water to make 100 mL of solution. Do this for each sugar solution used.	
	Yeast suspension	Mix 1 packet dry yeast with 100 mL water. Incubate for at least 10 minutes in 37°C water before the lab.	

Suppliers

Sources of Probeware

Vernier Software & Technology
13979 SW Millikan Way
Beaverton, OR 97005-2886
(888) 837-6437
info@vernier.com
www.vernier.com

Texas Instruments
Customer Support
P.O. Box 650311, MS 3962
Dallas, TX 75265
(800) 842-2737
ti-cares@ti.com
www.ti.com

PASCO Scientific
10101 Foothills Blvd.
P.O. Box 619011
Roseville, CA 95747-9011
(800) 772-8700
sales@pasco.com
www.pasco.com

Equipment Suppliers

American Science & Surplus
P.O. Box 1030
Skokie, IL 60076
1-847-647-0011
www.sciplus.com

Bio-Rad Laboratories
2000 Alfred Nobel Dr.
Life Science Group
Hercules, CA 94547
(800) 876-3425
www.biorad.com

Carolina Biological Supply Co.
2700 York Road
Burlington, NC 27215
(800) 334-5551
carolina.com

Edmund Scientifics
60 Pearce Ave.
Tonawanda, NY 14150-6711
(800) 728-6999
www.scientificsonline.com

Fisher Science Education
4500 Turnberry
Hanover Park, IL 60133
(800) 955-1177
fisheredu.com

Nasco Science
901 Janesville Avenue
P.O. Box 901
Fort Atkinson, WI 53538-0901
(800) 558-9595
www.nascofa.com

Nebraska Scientific
3823 Leavenworth St.
Omaha, NE 68105-1180
(800) 228-7117
nebraskascientific.com

PASCO Scientific
10101 Foothills Blvd.
Roseville, CA 95747-7100
(800) 772-8700
pasco.com

Sargent-Welch/VWR
Scientific Products
P.O. Box 5229
Buffalo Grove, IL 60089-5229
(800) SAR-GENT
www.sargentwelch.com

Ward's Natural Science Est.
5100 W. Henrietta Road
P.O. Box 92912
Rochester, NY 14692-9012
(800) 962-2660
www.wardsci.com

Contents

To the Student

The activities in this book are designed to help you study science using probeware technology. A probeware lab is different from other labs because it uses a probe or sensor to collect data, a data collection unit to interpret and store the data, and a graphing calculator or computer to analyze the data. These components are connected with a software program called DataMate that makes them work together in an easy-to-use, handheld system. These labs are designed specifically for the TI-73 or TI-83 Plus graphing calculators and a CBL 2™ (produced by Texas Instruments, Inc.) or Vernier LabPro® (produced by Vernier Software & Technology) data collection unit.

The activities in this book will help you improve your ability to recognize and use equipment properly and to analyze data. To help you get started, the next few pages will provide you with:

- information about **getting started with probeware**
- a list of **laboratory and safety guidelines**
- a reference page of **safety symbols**

Each lab activity in this manual includes the following sections:

- **Introduction**—The introductory paragraphs give you background information needed to understand the activity.
- **Objectives**—The list of objectives is a guide to what will be done in the activity and what will be expected of you.
- **Materials**—The materials section lists the supplies you will need to complete the activity.
- **Procedure**—The procedure gives you step-by-step instructions for carrying out the activity. Many steps have safety precautions. Be sure to read these statements and obey them for your own and your classmates' protection. Unless told to do otherwise, you are expected to complete all parts of each assigned activity. Important information needed for the procedure but that is not an actual procedural step is also found in this section.
- **Hypothesis**—You will develop a hypothesis statement to express your expectations of the results and as an answer to the problem statement.
- **Data and Observations**—This section includes tables and space to record data and observations.
- **Analysis**—In this section, you draw conclusions about the results of the activity just completed. Rereading the introduction before answering the questions is most helpful at this time.
- **Checking Your Hypothesis**—You will determine whether your data supports your hypothesis.
- **Further Investigations/Further Explorations**—This section gives ideas for further activities that you may do on your own. They may be either laboratory or library research.

Getting Started with Probeware

The following instructions will guide you through the setup process for the data collection unit and the graphing calculator. The activities are compatible with either the CBL 2 or the LabPro unit. Each activity was written for use with TI-73 or TI-83 Plus graphing calculators. These activities can be adapted for use with other graphing calculators or other data collection units, if desired.

Connecting a Graphing Calculator to the CBL 2 or LabPro Unit

1. Insert batteries into the CBL 2 or LabPro unit and graphing calculator.

2. The cradle is an optional accessory that conveniently connects the two units. Slide the back of the cradle onto the front of the CBL 2 or LabPro unit until it clicks into place.

3. Insert the upper end of the calculator into the cradle and press down on the lower end until it locks into place.

4. Connect the CBL 2 or LabPro unit to the graphing calculator using the unit-to-unit link cable. Plug the cable into the I/O port at the end of the CBL 2 or LabPro unit and the other end into the I/O port at the end of the calculator. Make sure that the unit-to-unit link cable is securely in place.

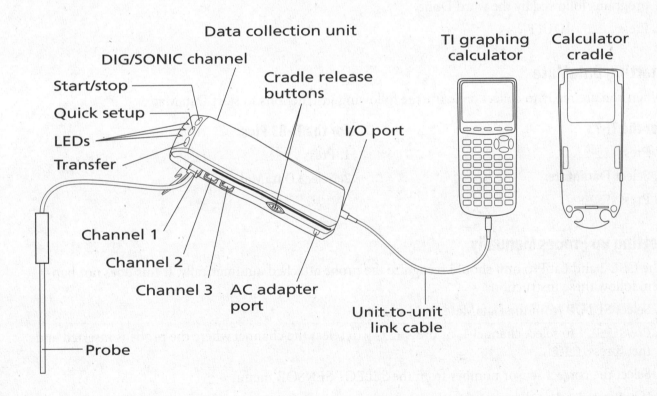

Resetting the Calculator Memory

It is recommended that the memory of the calculator be cleared before the DataMate data collection program is transferred.

1. Press `2nd` [MEM].

2. Select **Reset**.

3. Select **ALL RAM . . .**

4. Select **Reset**. The calculator screen will display **RAM cleared**.

Transferring DataMate to the Calculator

The DataMate program is stored on the CBL 2 or LabPro unit and is transferred to the graphing calculator for use. Once DataMate is transferred to the graphing calculator, it will remain there until the calculator memory is reset using the instructions above.

1. For the TI-73, press `APPS`. Select **Link . . .**

   For the TI-83 Plus, press `2nd` [LINK].

2. Use the right arrow to highlight **RECEIVE**. Press `ENTER`.

3. The screen will display **Waiting . . .** Press the large **TRANSFER** key found on the upper left-hand side of the CBL 2 or LabPro unit. When the transfer is complete, the screen will display the transferred programs followed by the word **Done**.

4. Press `2nd` [QUIT].

Starting DataMate

When you are ready to collect data, use the following instructions to start DataMate.

For the TI-73:

1. Press `PRGM`.

2. Select **DataMate**.

3. Press `ENTER`.

For the TI-83 Plus:

1. Press `APPS`.

2. Select **DataMate**.

Setting up Probes Manually

The CBL 2 and LabPro unit should recognize the probe attached automatically. If this does not happen, follow these instructions.

1. Select **SETUP** from the DataMate main screen.

2. Press `ENTER` to select channel 1, or press `▼` to select the channel where the probe is inserted and then press `ENTER`.

3. Select the correct sensor number from the SELECT SENSOR menu.

4. If requested, select the type of probe used.

5. Select **OK** to return to the DataMate main screen.

Laboratory and Safety Guidelines

Emergencies

- Inform the teacher immediately of *any* mishap—fire, injury, glassware breakage, chemical spills, and so forth.
- Know the location of the fire extinguisher, safety shower, eyewash, fire blanket, and first-aid kit. Know how to use this equipment.
- If chemicals come into contact with your eyes or skin, flush with large quantities of water and notify your teacher immediately.

Preventing Accidents

- Do NOT wear clothing that is loose enough to catch on anything. Do NOT wear sandals or open-toed shoes. Remove loose jewelry—chains or bracelets—while doing lab work.
- Wear protective safety gloves, goggles, and aprons as instructed.
- Always wear safety goggles (not glasses) in the laboratory.
- Wear goggles throughout the entire activity, cleanup, and handwashing.
- Keep your hands away from your face while working in the laboratory.
- Remove synthetic fingernails before working in the lab (these are highly flammable).
- Do NOT use hair spray, mousse, or other flammable hair products just before or during laboratory work where an open flame is used (they can ignite easily).
- Tie back long hair and loose clothing to keep them away from flames and equipment.
- Eating, drinking, chewing gum, applying makeup, and smoking are prohibited in the laboratory.
- Do NOT inhale vapors or taste, touch, or smell any chemical or substance unless instructed to do so by your teacher.

Working in the Laboratory

- Study all instructions before you begin a laboratory or field activity. Ask questions if you do not understand any part of the activity.
- Work ONLY on activities assigned by your teacher. NEVER work alone in the laboratory.
- Do NOT substitute other chemicals/substances for those listed in your activity.
- Do NOT begin any activity until directed to do so by your teacher.
- Do NOT handle any equipment without specific permission.
- Remain in your own work area unless given permission by your teacher to leave it.
- Do NOT point heated containers—test tubes, flasks, and so forth—at yourself or anyone else.
- Do NOT take any materials or chemicals out of the classroom.
- Stay out of storage areas unless you are instructed to be there and are supervised by your teacher.

Laboratory Cleanup

- Keep work, lab, and balance areas clean, limiting the amount of easily ignitable materials.
- Turn off all burners, water faucets, probeware, and calculators before leaving the lab.
- Carefully dispose of waste materials as instructed by your teacher.
- With your goggles on, wash your hands thoroughly with soap and warm water after each activity.

Safety Symbols

SAFETY SYMBOLS	HAZARD	EXAMPLES	PRECAUTION	REMEDY
DISPOSAL	Special disposal procedures need to be followed.	certain chemicals, living organisms	Do not dispose of these materials in the sink or trash can.	Dispose of wastes as directed by your teacher.
BIOLOGICAL	Organisms or other biological materials that might be harmful to humans	bacteria, fungi, blood, unpreserved tissues, plant materials	Avoid skin contact with these materials. Wear mask or gloves.	Notify your teacher if you suspect contact with material. Wash hands thoroughly.
EXTREME TEMPERATURE	Objects that can burn skin by being too cold or too hot	boiling liquids, hot plates, dry ice, liquid nitrogen	Use proper protection when handling.	Go to your teacher for first aid.
SHARP OBJECT	Use of tools or glassware that can easily puncture or slice skin	razor blades, pins, scalpels, pointed tools, dissecting probes, broken glass	Practice common-sense behavior and follow guidelines for use of the tool.	Go to your teacher for first aid.
FUME	Possible danger to respiratory tract from fumes	ammonia, acetone, nail polish remover, heated sulfur, moth balls	Make sure there is good ventilation. Never smell fumes directly. Wear a mask.	Leave foul area and notify your teacher immediately.
ELECTRICAL	Possible danger from electrical shock or burn	improper grounding, liquid spills, short circuits, exposed wires	Double-check setup with teacher. Check condition of wires and apparatus.	Do not attempt to fix electrical problems. Notify your teacher immediately.
IRRITANT	Substances that can irritate the skin or mucous membranes of the respiratory tract	pollen, moth balls, steel wool, fiberglass, potassium permanganate	Wear dust mask and gloves. Practice extra care when handling these materials.	Go to your teacher for first aid.
CHEMICAL	Chemicals that can react with and destroy tissue and other materials	bleaches such as hydrogen peroxide; acids such as sulfuric acid, hydrochloric acid; bases such as ammonia, sodium hydroxide	Wear goggles, gloves, and an apron.	Immediately flush the affected area with water and notify your teacher.
TOXIC	Substance may be poisonous if touched, inhaled, or swallowed.	mercury, many metal compounds, iodine, poinsettia plant parts	Follow your teacher's instructions.	Always wash hands thoroughly after use. Go to your teacher for first aid.
OPEN FLAME	Open flame may ignite flammable chemicals, loose clothing, or hair.	alcohol, kerosene, potassium permanganate, hair, clothing	Tie back hair. Avoid wearing loose clothing. Avoid open flames when using flammable chemicals. Be aware of locations of fire safety equipment.	Notify your teacher immediately. Use fire safety equipment if applicable.

Eye Safety
Proper eye protection should be worn at all times by anyone performing or observing science activities.

Clothing Protection
This symbol appears when substances could stain or burn clothing.

Animal Safety
This symbol appears when safety of animals and students must be ensured.

Radioactivity
This symbol appears when radioactive materials are used.

Lab 1 — Is oxygen cycled in the environment?

Plants and animals interact with each other in many ways. One of those ways is by cycling carbon. For example, animals release the carbon dioxide that is produced when their cells break down food. Plants take in the carbon dioxide and use it to make food during photosynthesis. One of the by-products of photosynthesis is oxygen. What happens to the oxygen that is produced by plants? Does it cycle between plants and animals? In this lab, you will design an experiment to find out, using a probe that measures the concentration of oxygen dissolved in water.

Problem

How could you find out whether oxygen is cycled between plants and animals in the environment? What would happen if you placed an aquatic plant and/or aquatic animal in a closed aquatic system, one in which gases could not enter or leave?

Hypothesis

Hypothesize whether oxygen is cycled between plants and animals in the environment. Write your hypothesis below.

_____

_____

Objectives

- Hypothesize whether oxygen is cycled between plants and animals in the environment.
- Design a closed aquatic system that does not allow gases to enter or leave.
- Interpret data to determine whether oxygen is cycled between plants and animals.

Possible Materials

- ❑ LabPro or CBL 2 interface
- ❑ TI graphing calculator
- ❑ LabPro or CBL 2 AC adapter (optional)
- ❑ link cable
- ❑ Vernier dissolved oxygen probe
- ❑ small, clear containers with caps, to be used for the closed systems

- ❑ aquatic animal, such as a snail
- ❑ aquatic plant, such as *Elodea*
- ❑ tap water (allowed to stand for one day)
- ❑ artificial light source
- ❑ D.O. electrode filling solution
- ❑ Beral pipette
- ❑ metric ruler

- ❑ 100-mL graduated cylinder
- ❑ 10-mL graduated cylinder
- ❑ 250-mL beakers
- ❑ distilled water
- ❑ wax marking pencil
- ❑ lab wipes
- ❑ laboratory apron
- ❑ goggles

Is oxygen cycled in the environment?,
continued

Plan the Experiment

1. Devise a procedure you can use to determine whether oxygen is cycled between plants and animals in an aquatic environment. The procedure should use a probeware system that includes a dissolved oxygen probe, LabPro or CBL 2 interface, TI graphing calculator, and link cable.

2. Decide on the type of closed system you will design and the number of closed systems you will need to observe in order to make valid conclusions. Decide on the variable that you will manipulate and those that you will keep constant.

3. Think about how long you will wait before taking measurements of the dissolved oxygen levels in the closed systems. Before you collect data, the probeware system including the dissolved oxygen probe must be set up, warmed up, and calibrated. Allow time in your experimental plan for these steps.

4. Write your procedure on another sheet of paper or in your notebook. It should include all the materials you will use.

   CAUTION: *To avoid harming the plants and animals, do not place the closed systems too close to an artificial light source. Heat from the light source may raise the water temperature above a safe level.*

Check the Plan

1. Be sure to include a control group for comparison purposes in your experiment. Do you have different combinations of organisms in the experimental groups?

2. Make sure the teacher has approved your experimental plan before you proceed further.

Carry Out Your Experiment

1. Follow the steps in your plan.

2. Connect the TI graphing calculator to the LabPro or CBL 2 interface using the link cable. Connect the dissolved oxygen probe

into Channel 1 of the interface. If the dissolved oxygen probe needs to be warmed up, proceed to Step 3. If the probe has already been warmed up, proceed to Step 7.

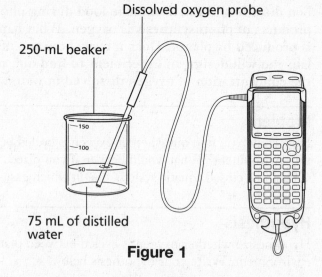

Figure 1

3. Set up the dissolved oxygen probe.

   a. Unscrew the membrane cap (counterclockwise) from the tip of the electrode on the dissolved oxygen probe. Do not touch the membrane at the very tip of the probe.

   b. Use a Beral pipette to fill the membrane cap with about 1 mL of D.O. electrode filling solution. Carefully thread the membrane cap (clockwise) onto the electrode body. Do not over tighten the cap. Rinse the electrode with distilled water and carefully wipe it dry with a lab wipe.

   c. Place the dissolved oxygen probe in a 250-mL beaker containing about 75 mL of distilled water.

4. Turn on the calculator and start the DATA-MATE program. Press CLEAR to reset the program.

5. The dissolved oxygen probe must be powered and connected to the LabPro or CBL 2 interface to be warmed up.

   a. If the calculator screen displays CH 1 DO (MG/L), proceed to Step 6. If it does not, continue with this step to manually select the dissolved oxygen probe.

Copyright © by Glencoe/McGraw-Hill, a division of the McGraw-Hill Companies, Inc.

b. Select SETUP from the main screen.

c. Press ENTER to select CH 1.

d. Select D. OXYGEN (MG/L) from the SELECT SENSOR menu.

e. Select OK to return to the main screen.

6. Warm up the dissolved oxygen probe for 10 minutes.

a. With the probe still in the water, wait 10 minutes while the probe warms up. The probe must stay connected to the interface at all times to keep it warmed up. If disconnected for a period longer than a few minutes, it will be necessary to warm it up again.

b. At the end of class, leave the dissolved oxygen probe connected to the interface, with the DATAMATE program running. If this is done, the probe will stay warm and ready for the next class.

7. NOTE: *Proceed with this part of the lab only after the dissolved oxygen probe has been warmed up.*

a. After the desired number of days has passed, open one of the closed systems, being careful not to agitate the water, which could cause a change in the amount of dissolved oxygen.

b. Slowly pour the water from the closed system into a 250-mL beaker, and then insert the dissolved oxygen probe into the water. Using a gentle swirling motion, stir the dissolved oxygen probe through the water. Make sure no bubbles are trapped under the tip of the probe. Liquid must be continually moving past the membrane of the electrode. Monitor the dissolved oxygen readings displayed on the calculator screen. Once the reading has stabilized, record the value in Table 1, or you can make your own data table. Rinse the end of the probe with distilled water before testing the water from another closed system.

c. Place the probe in a beaker of distilled water. Leave the DATAMATE program and calculator running for the next class.

d. If you are the last class to use the equipment, exit the DATAMATE program and turn off the calculator. Disconnect the probe from the LabPro or CBL 2. Remove the membrane cap and rinse the inside and outside of the cap with distilled water. Rinse and carefully dry the exposed cathode and anode inner elements of the probe. Reinstall the membrane cap loosely onto the electrode body for storage.

8. After doing the experiment, return the organisms to their original locations or follow the teacher's directions.

Data and Observations

Table 1

Descriptions of Closed Systems	Concentration of Dissolved Oxygen (ppm)

Lab 1 **Is oxygen cycled in the environment?,** **Probeware Activity**
continued

Analysis

1. Which closed system had the highest concentration of dissolved oxygen? Explain why.

_____

_____

_____

2. Which closed system had the lowest concentration of dissolved oxygen? Explain why.

_____

_____

_____

_____

3. From your data, what can you conclude about whether oxygen is cycled between plants and animals? Explain.

_____

_____

_____

_____

4. Why was it necessary to have a closed system in your experiment?

_____

_____

_____

_____

Checking Your Hypothesis

Was your hypothesis supported by your data? Why or why not?

_____

_____

_____

Further Investigations

1. Repeat the lab using different aquatic plants and/or animals. Compare your results from the two experiments.

2. Modify the lab to compare the dissolved oxygen levels for closed systems that have been placed in low-light environments or in the dark.

Lab 2 — An Environmental Limiting Factor

Just as canaries warned early coal miners of dangerous levels of gas, so are fish, plants, and other organisms important indicators of the health of water and soil environments. These organisms are affected by the acidity of water and soil. The acidity of a substance is measured on the pH scale. Acids have pH values lower than 7, while bases have pH values above 7. A substance with a pH of 7 is neutral, being neither acidic nor basic. The farther a pH value is from 7, the more acidic or basic the substance is.

In this lab, you will investigate pH as a limiting factor by measuring the pH of a variety of soil and water samples in your area. Fish generally do well in pH ranges of 6.7 to 8.5. When the pH drops below 5 or exceeds 9, most fish have difficulty surviving. Thus, pH is considered a limiting factor—an environmental factor that affects the ability of organisms to survive. The acidity of lake waters is affected by acid rain and by minerals that leach out of alkaline (basic) or acidic soils and drain into lakes. Organisms that live in soil also are sensitive to acidity levels. For example, rhododendrons and azaleas are acid loving and do well in soils of pH 4–5.

Objectives

- Use a pH sensor to measure pH.
- Measure and compare the pH of soil and water samples.
- Evaluate the pH of the samples as an environmental limiting factor.

Materials

❑ LabPro or CBL 2 unit
❑ TI graphing calculator
❑ link cable
❑ pH sensor
❑ 250-mL beakers (2)
❑ soil samples (3 or more)

❑ plastic bags (3 or more)
❑ large spoon
❑ distilled water
❑ water samples (3 or more)
❑ paper plates (3)
❑ mortar and pestle

❑ balance
❑ jars with lids (8)
❑ wax marking pencil
❑ plastic or rubber gloves
❑ laboratory apron
❑ goggles

Lab 2 — An Environmental Limiting Factor, *continued*

Procedure

Part A. Preparing Soil Samples

1. Several days before the lab, use a spoon to collect three or more soil samples, each approximately three square centimeters wide by two centimeters deep. Samples could be taken from a lawn, wooded area, wetland, or home garden. Place the samples in separate plastic bags. While collecting, record in Table 1 the kinds of plants growing in the soil. **CAUTION: *Wear protective gloves while collecting and handling soil samples.***

2. Break up the samples and let them dry on separate paper plates for several days.

3. Grind the dry soil for each sample with a mortar and pestle. Remove any plant material or rock.

4. For each sample, place about 30 grams of soil and 60 grams of distilled water into a jar. Close the jar, label the source of the soil, and shake the jar vigorously. Allow the water to stand overnight.

Part B. Preparing Water Samples

1. Before the lab, collect water samples in jars with lids. These should include samples of distilled water, ocean or saltwater, aquarium water, precipitation (rain or snow), drinking water, and stream, pond, or lake water. Label each jar by source. Then record the source of each sample in Table 2. **CAUTION: *Wear protective gloves while collecting and handling water samples.***

2. Store samples in a cool place. Allow snow or ice to melt at room temperature.

Part C. Preparing the pH Sensor

1. Plug the pH sensor into Channel 1 of the LabPro or CBL 2 interface. Using the link cable, connect the TI graphing calculator to the interface. Push the link cable securely into each jack.

2. Turn on the graphing calculator. Start the DATAMATE program and go to the MAIN MENU. Press CLEAR to reset the program. If the DATAMATE program is not loaded, transfer the program from the memory of the LabPro or CBL 2 interface to the TI graphing calculator.

3. Set up the calculator and interface for a pH Sensor.

   a. If the calculator displays PH in CH 1, proceed directly to Part D. If it does not, continue with this step to set up your sensor manually.

   b. Select SETUP from the main screen.

   c. Press ENTER to select CH 1.

   d. Select PH from the SELECT SENSOR menu.

   e. Select OK to return to the main screen. Readings from the pH sensor will be displayed on the main screen.

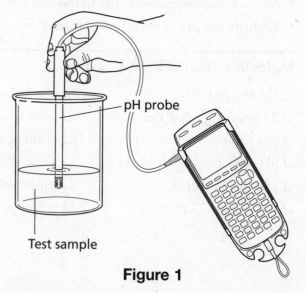

pH probe

Test sample

Figure 1

Lab 2 **An Environmental Limiting Factor,** *continued* **Probeware Activity**

Part D. Testing the Samples

1. Before each use of the pH sensor, hold it over a beaker and gently rinse the tip with distilled water. **CAUTION:** *The tip of the pH sensor can be broken easily.* Do not let the sensor dry out. When not in use, immerse the sensor in a beaker of tap water.

2. Pour a soil solution or water sample into a clean, dry beaker.

3. Carefully place the pH sensor in the beaker as shown in Figure 1. Allow the pH value reading to stabilize for 15–20 seconds. Record the value in Table 1 for a soil sample or in Table 2 for a water sample.

4. Dispose of the sample and rinse and dry the beaker.

5. Repeat Part D, steps 1–4, for your other samples.

6. At the conclusion of the lab, wash your hands thoroughly with soap and water.

7. Share your data with other class members.

Data and Observations

Table 1

Source of Soil Sample	Plants That Grow in This Soil	pH

Table 2

Source of Water Sample	pH

Lab 2 — An Environmental Limiting Factor, *continued*   **Probeware Activity**

Analysis

1. Compare the pH values of the soil and water samples. Which sample showed the highest pH value? The lowest pH value?

   _____

   _____

2. Did soils of differing pH levels support different types of plants? Explain.

   _____

   _____

3. Compare the pH values for the precipitation samples and for the samples from bodies of water. Summarize your observations.

   _____

   _____

   _____

4. How does the pH value of your drinking water compare with that of natural bodies of water and precipitation?

   _____

   _____

5. Which of the water samples you tested would provide the greatest limiting factor for fish?

   _____

   _____

   _____

Further Investigations

1. Contact a nursery or do research to determine how the soil pH in your area acts as a limiting factor for plants.

2. GLOBE (Global Learning and Observations to Benefit the Environment) is a worldwide network of students, teachers, and scientists working together to study and understand the global environment. Join the GLOBE schools to observe the archival data or atmospheric and hydrologic data. GLOBE students make environmental observations near their schools and report the data through the Internet. The GLOBE program is connected to NOAA, the National Atmospheric and Oceanic Administration.

Lab

3   Testing Water Quality

One way of judging water quality is to determine the amount of oxygen dissolved in the water. Oxygen may be supplied to a body of water from the air and from photosynthetic organisms living in the water. Clean water usually has a high oxygen content. Polluted water usually has a low oxygen content because organisms in the water use the oxygen as they decompose.

Objectives

- Using a dissolved oxygen probe, measure the concentration of dissolved oxygen in water samples obtained from different locations.

- Give reasons why the water samples have different concentrations of dissolved oxygen.

Materials

- ❏ LabPro or CBL 2 unit
- ❏ AC adapter (optional)
- ❏ TI graphing calculator
- ❏ link cable
- ❏ Vernier dissolved oxygen probe
- ❏ sodium sulfite calibration solution
- ❏ D.O. electrode filling solution

- ❏ Beral pipette
- ❏ dissolved oxygen calibration bottle
- ❏ metric ruler
- ❏ classroom thermometer
- ❏ classroom barometer
- ❏ water samples from different locations (4 or more)
- ❏ jars with lids (4 or more)

- ❏ plastic or rubber gloves
- ❏ 100-mL graduated cylinder
- ❏ 10-mL graduated cylinder
- ❏ 100-mL beakers (5)
- ❏ distilled water
- ❏ wax marking pencil
- ❏ lab wipes
- ❏ laboratory apron
- ❏ goggles

Procedure

Part A. Set up the Dissolved Oxygen Probe

1. Connect the TI graphing calculator to the LabPro or CBL 2 interface using the link cable. Connect the dissolved oxygen probe into Channel 1 of the interface. If the dissolved oxygen probe needs to be warmed up, proceed to Step 2. If the probe has already been warmed up, proceed to Part B.

2. Unscrew the membrane cap (counterclockwise) from the tip of the electrode on the dissolved oxygen probe. Do not touch the membrane at the very tip of the probe.

3. Use a Beral pipet to fill the membrane cap with about 1 mL of D.O. electrode filling solution. Carefully thread the membrane cap (clockwise) onto the electrode body. Do not over tighten the cap. Rinse the electrode with distilled water and carefully wipe it dry with a lab wipe.

4. Place the dissolved oxygen probe in a 250-mL beaker containing about 75 mL of water.

5. Turn on the calculator and start the DATA-MATE program. Press CLEAR to reset the program.

   a. If the calculator screen displays CH 1 DO (MG/L), proceed to Step 6. If it does not, continue with this step to manually select the dissolved oxygen probe.

   b. Select SETUP from the main screen.

   c. Press ENTER to select CH 1.

   d. Select D. OXYGEN (MG/L) from the SELECT SENSOR menu.

   e. Select OK to return to the main screen.

6. Warm up the dissolved oxygen probe for 10 minutes.

   a. With the probe still in the water, wait 10 minutes while the probe warms up. The probe must stay connected to the interface at all times to keep it warmed up. If disconnected for a period longer than a few minutes, it will be necessary to warm it up again.

   b. At the end of class, leave the dissolved oxygen probe connected to the interface, with the DATAMATE program running. If this is done, the probe will stay warm and ready for the next class.

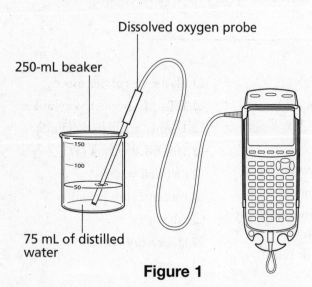

Dissolved oxygen probe
250-mL beaker
75 mL of distilled water

Figure 1

Part B. Calibrate the Dissolved Oxygen Probe

1. Select SETUP from the main screen.
2. Select CALIBRATE from the setup screen.
3. Select CALIBRATE NOW.
4. Determine the zero-oxygen calibration point.

   a. Remove the probe from the water and place the tip of the probe into the sodium sulfite calibration solution. **IMPORTANT:** *No air bubbles can be trapped below the tip of the probe or the probe will sense an inaccurate dissolved oxygen level.* If the voltage does not rapidly decrease, tap the side of the bottle with the probe to dislodge any bubbles. The readings should be in the 0.2- to 0.5-V range.

   b. When the voltage stabilizes (~1 minute), press ENTER .

   c. Enter "0" as the known concentration value in mg/L.

5. Determine the saturated DO calibration point.

   a. Rinse the probe with distilled water and gently blot dry.

   b. Unscrew the lid of the calibration bottle provided with the probe. Slide the lid and the grommet about 2 cm onto the probe body.

   c. Add water to the bottle to a depth of about 1 cm and screw the bottle into the cap, as shown. **IMPORTANT:** *Do not touch the membrane or get it wet during this step.*

   d. Keep the probe in this position for about a minute. The readings should be above 2.0 V. When the voltage stabilizes, press ENTER .

   e. Enter the correct saturated dissolved-oxygen value (in mg/L), from the Appendix on page 41, (for example, "8.66") using the current barometric pressure and air temperature values.

   f. Select OK to return to the setup screen.

   g. Select OK again to return to the main screen.

   h. Return the dissolved oxygen probe to the beaker of water.

Part C. Finding the Dissolved Oxygen Concentration of Various Water Samples

NOTE: *Proceed with this part of the lab only after the dissolved oxygen probe has been warmed up and calibrated.*

1. In jars, collect four or more water samples from different locations. Samples could come from a tap, a pond, a lake, a river, a puddle, or an aquarium. Try to find water that has been standing and has some algae growth. Fill the jars to the top, label by source, and seal with lids. **CAUTION:** *Wear protective gloves while collecting and handling water samples.* Record your observations of the water samples in Table 1. Indicate whether any look polluted or dirty.

Lab 3   Testing Water Quality, *continued*

2. With the water samples at room temperature, gently pour 25 mL of each into separate 100-mL beakers labeled with each source. Pour slowly to avoid making bubbles.

3. Set up the calculator for data collection. Select SETUP from the main screen. Select MODE by pressing ⬆ once and then pressing ENTER. Select SINGLE POINT from the SELECT MODE menu. Select OK to return to the main screen.

4. Using a gentle motion, stir the dissolved oxygen probe through the water in one of the beakers. Make sure no bubbles are trapped under the tip of the probe. To provide an accurate reading, liquid must be continually moving past the membrane of the electrode. Once the reading displayed on the calculator screen has stabilized, select START to collect data. When data collection finishes, the dissolved oxygen concentration of the sample will be displayed on the screen.

Record the concentration in Table 1. Press ENTER to return to the main screen. Rinse the end of the probe with distilled water and place it in the next beaker to be tested.

5. Repeat Step 4 for the other water samples.

6. When finished, place the probe in a beaker of distilled water. Leave the DATAMATE program and calculator running for the next class. If you are the last class to use the equipment, exit the DATAMATE program and turn off the calculator. Disconnect the probe from the LabPro or CBL 2. Remove the membrane cap and rinse the inside and outside of the cap with distilled water. Rinse and carefully dry the exposed cathode and anode inner elements of the probe. Reinstall the membrane cap loosely onto the electrode body for storage.

7. At the conclusion of the lab, wash your hands thoroughly with soap and water.

Data and Observations

Table 1

Sample	Water Source	Observations of Water	Concentration of Dissolved Oxygen (ppm)
1			
2			
3			
4			

Analysis

1. Explain why the water samples you collected have different concentrations of dissolved oxygen.

_____

_____

_____

2. A lake sample having less than 4 ppm of dissolved oxygen is harmful to aquatic life.
   a. Which of your samples could not support aquatic life?

_____

_____

   b. Explain why oxygen dissolved in water is important for aquatic life.

_____

_____

3. The graph in Figure 2 shows the values for dissolved oxygen in a lake at various depths. Explain what might cause the differences in the concentrations of dissolved oxygen.

_____

_____

_____

_____

_____

Figure 2

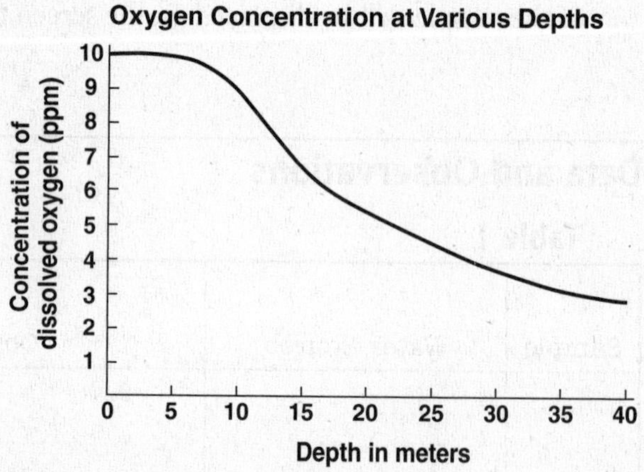

Oxygen Concentration at Various Depths

4. List errors you may have made in Part C that could have affected your results.

_____

_____

_____

Further Investigations

1. Put an aquatic plant in one water sample for a day and place the sample near a window. Determine the concentration of dissolved oxygen in the water at the beginning and end of the day, using the procedure in this lab. Explain any changes in the concentration of dissolved oxygen.

2. Place the water sample containing the plant in the dark for 48 hours. Find the concentration of dissolved oxygen at the beginning and end of this period. Explain any changes.

Lab 4 How well does yeast ferment different sugars?

The most commonly used yeast, *Saccharomyces cerevisiae*, is used as baker's yeast. The function of yeast in baking is to ferment sugars found in the flour or added to the dough. This fermentation gives off carbon dioxide and ethanol. The carbon dioxide is trapped in the dough, forming gas bubbles. As the gas in the bubbles expands, the dough stretches, or rises. The baking process kills the yeast and causes the ethanol to evaporate from the dough.

In this lab, you will design an experiment to test how well yeast ferments different sugars. The amount of carbon dioxide given off by the yeast is proportional to the amount of sugar that is fermented by the yeast. The amount of carbon dioxide produced can be measured with a carbon dioxide gas sensor.

Problem
Does yeast ferment different sugars equally well, or does yeast ferment some sugars better than others?

Hypothesis
Write a hypothesis about whether yeast ferments some sugars better than others.

_____

_____

Objectives
- Hypothesize whether yeast ferments some sugars betters than others.
- Using a carbon dioxide gas sensor, measure the amount of carbon dioxide gas produced by the fermentation of different sugars by yeast.
- Compare how well yeast ferments different sugars.

Possible Materials
- LabPro or CBL 2 unit
- carbon dioxide sensor
- TI graphing calculator
- link cable
- AC adapter (optional)
- different kinds of sugar solutions, such as glucose, sucrose (table sugar), fructose, dextrose, maltose, lactose
- yeast suspension
- test tube
- stirring rod
- 10-mL graduated cylinder
- thermometer
- water bath
- hot and cold water
- container for fermentation chamber
- clock or watch with second hand
- thermal mitts
- laboratory apron
- goggles

How well does yeast ferment different sugars?, *continued*

Plan the Experiment

1. Decide on a procedure that you can use to compare how well yeast ferments different sugars. The procedure should include a probeware system consisting of a carbon dioxide gas sensor, LabPro or CBL 2 interface, graphing calculator, and link cable. Other possible materials are listed on the previous page.

2. Prepare a water bath to incubate the yeast suspension. The temperature of the water bath should be maintained at a constant temperature of around 37°C.

3. Design a fermentation chamber in which the yeast will ferment the sugar.

4. Decide which sugars you will test. Think about how much yeast suspension and sugar solution you will use. After mixing the yeast suspension with the sugar solution, allow the mixture to incubate at 37°C for 10 minutes before adding it to the fermentation chamber.

5. Observe the mixture in the fermentation chamber. Use caution when placing the carbon dioxide probe into the fermentation chamber. Twist the stopper slightly to seal it in the opening being careful not to twist the shaft of the sensor. Use the carbon dioxide sensor to collect data on the amount of carbon dioxide gas produced from the fermentation of the sugar by the yeast.

6. To collect data, start the DATAMATE program and go to the MAIN MENU. Press CLEAR to reset the program. If the DATAMATE program is not loaded, transfer the program from the memory of the LabPro or CBL 2 interface to the TI graphing calculator. Do not select START until you are ready to collect data from the sensor in the fermentation chamber.

7. Decide how frequently you will collect data and for how long. You can record your observations and data in the tables provided or make your own tables. Label the columns appropriately.

8. Write your procedure on another sheet of paper or in your notebook. It should include the amounts of each material you will need.

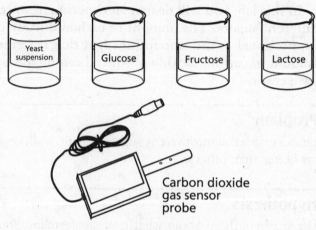

Figure 1

Check the Plan

1. Be sure that you include a control fermentation chamber in your experiment and that the experimental fermentation chambers vary in one way only.

2. Make sure your teacher has approved your experimental plan before you proceed further.

3. Carry out the experiment.

4. As you do the experiment, keep the water bath at 37°C.

5. Completely rinse the fermentation chamber with water after each trial to remove used sugar, yeast, and carbon dioxide. Thoroughly dry the inside with a paper towel. Fan the carbon dioxide sensor with air after each trial. This will clear the sensor of any excess carbon dioxide.

Data and Observations

Table 1

Type of Sugar in Chamber	Observations

Table 2

Time (in seconds)	Carbon Dioxide Concentration (ppm)			
	Sugar used: _____	Sugar used: _____	Sugar used: _____	Sugar used: _____

Table 3

Type of Sugar Used	Rate of Fermentation (ppm/s)

Analysis

1. Use the graphing calculator to graph carbon dioxide concentration (ppm) versus time for the control trial and for each sugar trial.

   a. Select ANALYZE from the main screen.

   b. Select CURVE FIT from the ANALYZE OPTIONS menu.

   c. Select LINEAR (CH 1 VS TIME) from the CURVE FIT menu.

   d. The linear-regression statistics for these two lists are displayed for the equation in the form:
   $$Y = A \cdot X + B$$

   e. Enter the value of the slope, A, as the rate of fermentation in Table 3.

   f. Press ENTER to view a graph of the data and the regression line.

   g. Press ENTER to return to the ANALYZE menu.

   h. Select RETURN TO MAIN SCREEN from the ANALYZE menu. Repeat the procedure for each trial.

2. How well did the yeast ferment the different sugars?

   _____

3. What is a possible explanation for your answer to question 2?

   _____

4. Why was it important to keep the water bath in which the yeast was incubated at 37°C?

   _____

5. What variables did you keep constant in your experiment?

   _____

6. Explain the data you recorded for the control fermentation chamber.

   _____

Checking Your Hypothesis

Was your hypothesis supported by your data? Why or why not?

_____

_____

Further Investigations

1. Repeat the lab using different types of baker's yeast, such as dry yeast, cake yeast, and quick-starting yeast. Compare the fermentation rates of the different yeasts.

2. Research the genome map of yeast and present this information to the class.

Lab 5

How can pH be used to compare rates of photosynthesis?

During respiration, aquatic plants, such as *Elodea*, release carbon dioxide into the water. During photosynthesis, the plants extract the carbon dioxide they need from the water. Carbon dioxide dissolves in water to form a weak acid called carbonic acid (H_2CO_3). Some of the carbonic acid dissociates to form H^+ ions and HCO_3^- ions, as shown below.

$$CO_2 + H_2O \leftrightarrows H_2CO_3$$
$$H_2CO_3 \leftrightarrows H^+ + HCO_3^-$$

The double direction arrows indicate that the chemical reactions can proceed in either direction, and thus are reversible. As the carbon dioxide concentration in water decreases, the concentration of carbonic acid also decreases, which increases the pH of the water. Conversely, an increase in the water's carbon dioxide concentration results in a decrease in pH. Therefore, the pH of water can be used as an indication of the level of photosynthesis of aquatic plants. The greater the rate of photosynthesis, the greater the amount of dissolved carbon dioxide used, and thus the higher the pH of the water. In this lab, you will design an experiment to test the effect of light intensity on the photosynthetic rate of an aquatic plant, using a probe that measures pH.

Problem

Do plants undergo different rates of photosynthesis at different times of the day? Do plants undergo different rates of photosynthesis in different parts of the ocean? How does light intensity affect the rate of photosynthesis of plants?

Hypothesis

Write a hypothesis about the effect of light intensity on the rate of photosynthesis of aquatic plants.

_____

_____

Objectives

- Make a hypothesis about the effect of light intensity on the rate of photosynthesis.
- Expose an aquatic plant to different intensities of light.
- Use a probe to measure the pH of water samples.
- Compare the rates of photosynthesis of an aquatic plant exposed to different light intensities.

Lab 5 — How can pH be used to compare rates of photosynthesis?, *continued*

Possible Materials 🥽 📋 🧹

- ❏ LabPro or CBL 2 unit
- ❏ TI graphing calculator
- ❏ link cable
- ❏ AC adapter (optional)
- ❏ pH sensor

- ❏ aquatic plant, such as *Elodea*
- ❏ large test tubes with stoppers
- ❏ test-tube rack
- ❏ various light sources
- ❏ dechlorinated water

- ❏ rinse bottle of distilled water
- ❏ 250-mL beaker
- ❏ laboratory apron
- ❏ goggles

Plan The Experiment

1. Decide on a procedure that you can use to compare the rates of photosynthesis of an aquatic plant exposed to different intensities of light. The procedure should use a probeware system that includes a pH probe, LabPro or CBL 2 interface, TI graphing calculator, and link cable. You may wish to use the other suggested materials as well.

2. Think about how you will vary light intensity. How many samples will you test? Decide on the variables that you will need to keep constant during the experiment. What will be your control? **CAUTION:** *To avoid harming the aquatic plants you will be working with, do not place the samples too close to an artificial light source. Heat from the light source may increase the temperature of the water above the plant's tolerance level.*

3. Decide how frequently you will collect data and for how long. To collect data, plug the pH sensor into Channel 1 of the LabPro or CBL 2 interface. Using the link cable, connect the TI graphing calculator to the interface. Push the link cable securely into each jack.

4. Turn on the graphing calculator. Start the DATAMATE program and go to the MAIN MENU. Press CLEAR to reset the program. If the DATAMATE program is not loaded, transfer the program from the memory of the LabPro or CBL 2 interface to the TI graphing calculator.

5. Set up the calculator and interface for a pH sensor.

    a. If the calculator displays PH in CH 1, proceed directly to Step 6. If it does not, continue with this step to set up your sensor manually.

    b. Select SETUP from the main screen.

    c. Press ENTER to select CH 1.

    d. Select PH from the SELECT SENSOR menu.

    e. Select OK to return to the main screen. Readings from the pH sensor will be displayed on the main screen.

6. Before each use of the pH probe, rinse the tip of the electrode completely with distilled water. Carefully hold the pH probe over a beaker and use a rinse bottle to gently rinse the tip with distilled water. **CAUTION:** *The tip of the pH probe is fragile and can be broken easily.* Do not let the probe dry out. When not in use during the lab, keep the probe immersed in a beaker of tap water.

7. Place the probe in the sample. Allow the pH value reading to stabilize for 15 to 20 seconds. Record the value in Table 1, or you can make your own data table.

8. Write your procedure on another sheet of paper or in your notebook. It should include all the materials you will use.

Lab 5 How can pH be used to compare rates of photosynthesis?, *continued*

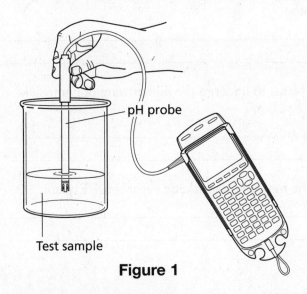

pH probe

Test sample

Figure 1

Check The Plan

1. Be sure that light intensity is the only variable that changes in your experiment.
2. Did you measure the pH of your samples before beginning the experiment?
3. Make sure the teacher has approved your experimental plan before you proceed further.
4. Carry out your experiment.
5. After the experiment, return the plants to their original location or as directed by the teacher.

Data and Observations

Table 1

pH of Samples			
Day	Type of light intensity: _____	Type of light intensity: _____	Type of light intensity: _____

Analysis

1. What variables did you keep constant in your experiment?

_____

_____

2. Which sample had the highest pH? The lowest pH?

_____

_____

3. Explain the differences in the pH values of the samples.

_____

_____

4. During what time of day would you expect outdoor plants to undergo the highest rate of photosynthesis? Explain.

_____

_____

5. In what part of the ocean would you expect to find the most photosynthetic organisms? Explain.

_____

_____

Checking Your Hypothesis

Was your hypothesis supported by your data? Why or why not?

_____

_____

_____

_____

Further Investigations

1. Repeat the experiment to investigate how the color of light affects the rate of photosynthesis.

2. Repeat the experiment devising a method to investigate whether temperature has an effect on the rate of photosynthesis.

Lab 6

Probeware Activity

Effect of Environmental Temperature on the Metabolic Rates of Animals

Endothermic (warm-blooded) animals, such as mammals, have the ability to maintain a constant internal body temperature through metabolic activity, but ectothermic (cold-blooded) animals do not. They do not generate much heat through their metabolism, so they must pick up heat from their environments. An ectothermic animal controls its internal temperature through its behavior. It may bask in the sun to get warmer or burrow underground to cool off. Ectothermic animals are more active in warm temperatures, and they slow down when the environment becomes cold. The rate of their activity can be examined by determining their metabolic rate. Animals consume food and break it down, producing carbon dioxide in the process of respiration. The overall reaction can be summarized by the following equation:

$$C_6H_{12}O_6 + 6O_2 \rightarrow 6CO_2 + 6H_2O + energy$$

The rate of carbon dioxide production can be used as a measure of the metabolic rate.

In this lab, you will be studying the relationship between the temperature of the environment and the metabolic rate of ectothermic animals. You will be able to monitor metabolic rate by measuring the carbon dioxide production during respiration, using a carbon dioxide gas sensor.

Objectives

- Use a carbon dioxide gas sensor to measure carbon dioxide concentrations.
- Determine the metabolic rate of small animals by measuring their rate of carbon dioxide production.
- Explain the effect of temperature on the metabolic rate of cold-blooded animals.

Materials 🥽 🧤 ✂️ 📋

- ❏ LabPro or CBL 2 unit
- ❏ TI graphing calculator
- ❏ link cable
- ❏ carbon dioxide sensor
- ❏ 250-mL respiration chamber (comes with sensor)
- ❏ thermometer
- ❏ crickets or pill bugs (4–10)
- ❏ warm tap water
- ❏ ice
- ❏ 500-mL or 1000-mL beaker
- ❏ Beral pipette or small beaker
- ❏ balance
- ❏ paper towels
- ❏ laboratory apron
- ❏ goggles

Effect of Environmental Temperature on the Metabolic Rates of Animals, *continued*

Procedure

To divide up the work for this lab, lab teams can work in three groups to test the same type of animal at different temperatures. Group One should collect data using temperatures at intervals between 10 and 20°C. Group Two should collect data using temperatures at intervals between 20 and 30°C. Group Three should collect data using temperatures at intervals between 30 and 40°C. Although the three groups will be using different individual animals that may differ in mass, the slight differences in mass of the animals should not make a significant difference in the results. An individual animal with greater mass should produce carbon dioxide at a higher rate, but we will assume that the rate will be proportional to its difference in mass. The carbon dioxide production rate, measured in ppm of CO_2/gram of animal mass, will be computed. At the conclusion of the lab, the three lab groups should share data.

1. Connect the LabPro or CBL 2 unit and TI graphing calculator with a link cable. Be sure to press the cable firmly into each piece of equipment. Connect the carbon dioxide sensor into CH 1 of the LabPro or CBL 2.

2. Turn on the graphing calculator and start the DATAMATE program. Press CLEAR to reset the program.

3. Set up the calculator and interface for a CO_2 gas sensor.

   a. Select SETUP from the main screen.

   b. If the calculator displays CO2 GAS (PPM) in CH 1, proceed directly to Step 4. If it does not, continue with this step to set up your sensor manually.

   c. Press ENTER to select CH 1.

   d. Select CO2 GAS from the SELECT SENSOR menu.

   e. Select parts per million (PPM) as the unit.

4. Set up the data collection parameters.

   a. Press ▲ once and then press ENTER to select MODE.

   b. Select TIME GRAPH from the MODE menu.

   c. Select CHANGE TIME SETTINGS from the TIME GRAPH SETTINGS menu.

   d. Enter "10" as the time between samples in seconds.

   e. Enter "60" as the number of samples to be collected.

   f. Select OK to return to the setup screen.

   g. Select OK to return to the main screen.

5. Prepare a water bath according to your assigned temperature.

   • **Group 1:** To prepare a 10 to 20°C water bath, place cool tap water in the 1000-mL beaker, add ice, and mix. Measure the temperature of the mixture. Add ice or cool water and mix until the water reaches the desired temperature.

   • **Group 2:** To prepare a 20 to 30°C water bath, start with warmer tap water and cool it with ice as needed.

   • **Group 3:** To prepare a 30 to 40°C water bath, start with warmer tap water and warm it with hot water as needed.

6. Measure the mass of your respiration chamber. Place your animals in the respiration chamber, and measure the mass of the respiration chamber again. **CAUTION: *Handle live animals with care.*** Calculate the difference between your measurements to find the mass of your animals. Record the mass of the animals in Table 1.

7. Carefully put the carbon dioxide probe into the top of the respiration chamber. Twist the stopper slightly to seat it in the opening. Be careful not to twist the shaft of the sensor. Place the respiration chamber in the water bath as shown in Figure 1. This setup will keep the animals at a constant temperature throughout the lab.

8. Wait five minutes to allow the temperature of the respiration chamber to adjust to the water bath temperature. Measure and record the water bath temperature in Table 1.

Lab 6 — Effect of Environmental Temperature on the Metabolic Rates of Animals, *continued*

Select START from the main screen to begin data collection. While data is being collected, try to maintain a constant temperature in your water bath.

9. When data collection has finished, a graph of CO2 GAS vs. TIME will be displayed. Press ENTER to return to the main screen.

10. Calculate the rate of respiration.

    a. Select ANALYZE from the main screen.

    b. Select CURVE FIT from the ANALYZE OPTIONS menu.

    c. Select LINEAR (CH 1 VS TIME) from the CURVE FIT menu.

    d. The best-fit line for your data is displayed in the form: $Y = A \cdot X + B$

    e. Enter the value of the slope, A, as the rate of carbon dioxide production in your data table.

    f. Press ENTER to view a graph of the data and the regression line.

    g. Press ENTER to return to the ANALYZE menu.

    h. Select RETURN TO MAIN SCREEN from the ANALYZE menu.

11. Remove the respiration chamber from the water bath. Dry off the respiration chamber and place it on the lab table. Carefully remove the carbon dioxide probe from the respiration chamber.

12. After all the data has been collected, place your animals in the location designated by your teacher. Exit the DATAMATE program and turn off the calculator. Share your data with the other lab groups.

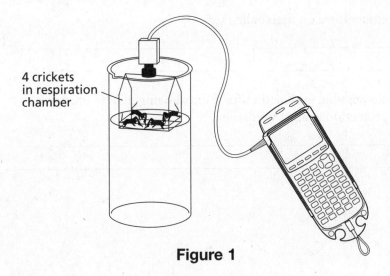

4 crickets in respiration chamber

Figure 1

Data and Observations

Animal Type _____

Table 1

Group	Animal Mass (g)	Temperature (°C)	CO$_2$ Production Rate (ppm/s)	CO$_2$ Production Rate per gram (ppm/s·g)
1				
2				
3				

Lab 6

Effect of Environmental Temperature on the Metabolic Rates of Animals, *continued*

Probeware Activity

Analysis

1. Determine the rate of CO_2 produced per gram of animal mass. Divide the CO_2 production rate by the animal mass. Record the CO_2 production rate per gram in Table 1.

2. Plot a graph of CO_2 production rate per gram versus temperature, plotting the CO_2 production rate (ppm/s · g) on the *y*-axis and temperature (°C) on the *x*-axis.

3. Compare the carbon dioxide production rates at the various temperatures tested. At what temperatures was the production rate of carbon dioxide the lowest and the highest?

4. What can you infer about the effect of temperature on metabolic rate?

5. Lizards are ectothermic animals. Suggest a possible explanation for a lizard being able to change its skin color other than for camouflage as protection against predators.

Further Explorations

1. Repeat the experiment with different types of animals such as cockroaches, flies, pill bugs, or mealworms. Compare the respiration rates for these animals.
2. Do research to find out more about the ways that ectothermic animals control their internal body temperature through behavior.

Name Date Class

Lab 7

Probeware Activity

What is the effect of exercise on body temperature?

The normal body temperature of a human is about 37°C. Normal metabolic processes generate heat that warms the body. The rate of heat production can be increased or decreased by a change in muscle activity or by hormonal action that changes metabolic rate. Sweating and the dilation of blood vessels help to cool the body when it becomes overheated. Shivering and the constriction of blood vessels help to warm the body when it becomes too cold. In this lab, you will design an experiment to test the effect of exercise on a person's body surface temperature. To monitor the temperature, you will attach a temperature probe to the skin.

Problem

How does exercise affect body surface temperature?

Hypothesis

Hypothesize how exercise affects a person's body surface temperature. Write your hypothesis on the lines below.

____

____

Objectives

- Hypothesize about the effect of exercise on body surface temperture.
- Measure body surface temperature using a temperature probe.
- Compare body surface temperature while at rest with body surface temperature while exercising.

Materials

- ❑ LabPro or CBL 2 unit
- ❑ TI graphing calculator
- ❑ link cable
- ❑ temperature probe
- ❑ athletic tape
- ❑ material for insulating the temperature probe, such as wool or polyester fill
- ❑ plastic bag to cover the temperature probe
- ❑ laboratory apron
- ❑ goggles

Lab 7

What is the effect of exercise on body temperature?, *continued*

Plan the Experiment

1. Decide on a procedure that you can use to test the effects of exercise on body surface temperature. The procedure should use a probeware system that includes a temperature probe, LabPro or CBL 2 interface, and TI graphing calculator.

2. As you develop your procedure, think about where on the body you will measure surface temperature. You might measure the surface temperature in different locations on the body before choosing a location to monitor while exercising. You can use Table 1 to record your resting-temperature data, or make your own table.

3. Choose an exercise that is safe for you to do. **CAUTION:** *If you have any conditions that may be aggravated by exercise, inform the teacher.*

4. Cover the temperature probe with a plastic bag to prevent sweat from getting on the probe.

5. Think about how often you will collect data while exercising and for how long. What will be your control? To collect data, set up the probeware system by connecting the link cable between the graphing calculator and the LabPro or CBL 2 interface. Firmly press the cable into each unit. Plug the temperature probe into Channel 1 of the interface. Turn on the calculator and start the DATAMATE program. Press CLEAR to reset the program.

6. Place the probe against the skin in the selected location. If part of the probe is exposed to the air, cover that part with an insulating material.

7. Temperature can be continuously monitored or collected for a specific amount of time. The current temperature readings are displayed on the calculator screen and updated once a second. If you wish to collect data for a period of time, select START. The DATA-MATE program will collect temperature readings for 180 seconds. If you wish to collect data for a longer time, select SETUP

from the main screen. Press [▲] to select MODE and press ENTER . Select TIME GRAPH from the MODE menu. Select CHANGE TIME SETTINGS from the TIME GRAPH menu. Enter how often you want data collected and how many points you wish to collect. To return to the main screen, select OK from the TIME GRAPH and SETUP menu. Select START when you want to begin data collection.

8. When data collection has finished, the calculator will display the graph of temperature versus time. After you are done looking at the graph, press ENTER to return to the main screen. Exit the program and press STAT then select EDIT to view your data. The time values will be in list L1 and the temperature readings will be in list L2. You can record selected data in Table 2, or make your own table.

9. Write your procedure on another sheet of paper or in your notebook. It should include any types of exercise equipment you will use.

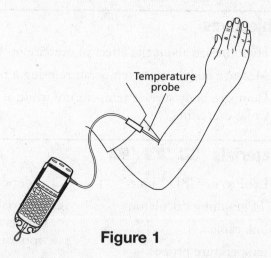

Temperature probe

Figure 1

Check the Plan

1. Your experiment should include a control.

2. Choose an exercise that is safe. Be sure that the exercise causes little disruption to other groups in the classroom.

3. Make sure the teacher has approved your experimental plan before you proceed further.

4. Carry out your experiment.

Lab 7   What is the effect of exercise on body temperature?, *continued*

Data and Observations

Table 1

Resting Temperatures	
Body location	Temperature (°C)

Table 2

Exercise Temperatures

Body location:

Type of exercise:

Time (seconds)	Temperature (°C)

Lab 7 — What is the effect of exercise on body temperature?, *continued*

Analysis

1. Describe the control in your experiment. What was its purpose?

_____

_____

2. Why might some parts of the body have a higher surface temperature than others?

_____

_____

3. What is the effect of exercise on body surface temperature? Why do you think exercise has this effect?

_____

_____

4. Explain the effect of the body's cooling mechanisms, such as blood-vessel dilation and sweating, on the data you obtained.

_____

_____

5. Would your data have differed if you had worn insulating clothing while exercising? Explain.

_____

_____

Checking Your Hypothesis

Was your hypothesis supported by your data? Why or why not?

_____

_____

_____

_____

Further Investigations

1. Repeat the experiment. This time collect body surface temperature data over a longer period of time and monitor the skin for sweating and a flushed appearance. Compare the temperature data you collect with those obtained in the first experiment.

2. Test the effects of different exercises on body surface temperature. Do some exercises affect body temperature more than others? If so, why?

Lab
8 Measuring Response Time

If you were walking down the street and heard someone call your name, it would take you a short time to look up, determine where the sound came from, and respond by waving. This interval of time is called your response time. You need time to perceive and process any stimulus, whether it is something you see, smell, feel, taste, or hear. For this lab, you will determine the time it takes you to respond to a sound stimulus.

Objectives

- Use a motion detector to determine the time it takes for a person to respond after hearing a sound.
- Conduct repeated trials and calculate an average response time.
- Compare the response times of different individuals.

Materials

- C-clamp
- LabPro or CBL 2 unit
- TI graphing calculator
- link cable
- motion detector

Procedure

1. Connect the LabPro or CBL 2 unit to the TI graphing calculator, using the link cable. Connect the motion detector to the DIG/SONIC 1 port on the right side of the interface. Place the motion detector about 4 meters from a blank wall, facing the wall, as shown in Figure 1.

2. Turn on the calculator and start the DATAMATE program. Press CLEAR to reset the program. If the program has not been loaded on the graphing calculator, transfer the program from the memory of the LabPro or CBL 2.

3. One of the students in the group will serve as the runner. That student should stand at the position shown in Figure 1, about 2 meters from the motion detector and slightly to one side. When data collection begins, the motion detector will transmit ultrasonic sound waves toward the wall. The runner should start outside of the range of the beam.

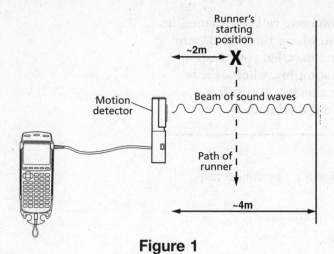

Figure 1

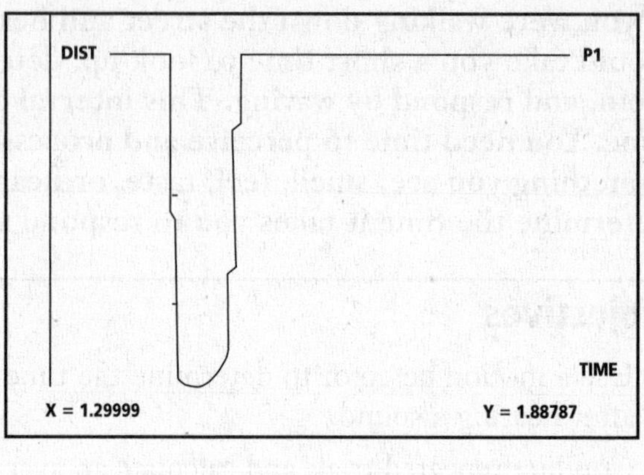

DIST   P1

TIME

X = 1.29999   Y = 1.88787

Figure 2

4. Another student will serve as the operator of the calculator and motion detector. The operator will select START to begin collecting data for the activity.

5. The motion detector makes a clicking sound once it begins emitting sound waves. As soon as the runner hears the clicking sound, he or she will run across the beam of the motion detector, as shown in Figure 1. Since the experiment seeks to measure the runner's response time to the sound, the runner should not run in response to visual stimuli. For that reason, the runner should not look at the operator or at the motion detector, since some models have an LED that becomes lit when the motion detector is on.

6. For 5 seconds after the motion detector has been turned on, the calculator will collect data. When data collection has finished, press ENTER to display a graph of distance vs. time. The graph may look like that shown in Figure 2. The horizontal part of the line indicates that the motion detector is bouncing sound waves off the wall, a stationary object. The depression in the line indicates that the sound waves have bounced off something closer to the detector—the runner as he or she ran across the beam.

7. Use the arrow keys on the calculator to trace along the curve until it gets to the lowest part of the depression. This point represents the time at which the runner crossed the beam. The x-value and y-value for that point will show on the screen. The x-value is the response time, or the time it took for the student to respond to the clicking of the motion detector and move across the beam. The y-value at this point indicates the distance between the motion detector and the runner. Record the x-value in Table 1 of Data and Observations, in the space for Trial 1.

8. When you are done working with the graph on the graphing calculator, press ENTER . Select MAIN SCREEN from the graph menu and repeat Steps 3–8 to collect more data. Every student in the group should be tested, and each student should do at least 5 trials. Make sure each student starts in the same position and that the motion detector is held in the same position for all of the trials. Copy the graph for one of your trials onto the grid in Data and Observations. (If you can print the LCD screen using TI-GRAPH LINK™, you can do that instead.)

9. When you have finished collecting data for all students in the group, select QUIT from the main screen and turn off the graphing calculator.

Lab 8 **Measuring Response Time,** *continued*

Probeware Activity

Data and Observations

Table 1

Trial	Response Time (seconds)				
	Student #1 Age:	Student #2 Age:	Student #3 Age:	Student #4 Age:	Student #5 Age:
1					
2					
3					
4					
5					
Average					

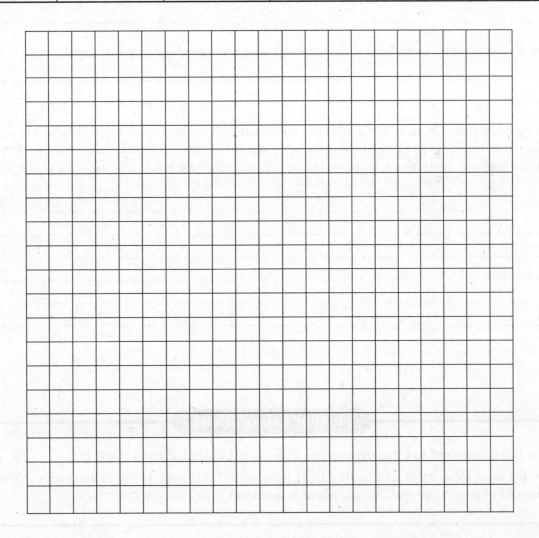

Analysis

1. Which student had the fastest response time in your group?

_____

_____

2. Did response times improve as more trials were done? Explain why you think improvement did or did not occur.

_____

_____

_____

_____

3. Was there any difference in the response time of students of different ages?

_____

_____

4. How do you think distance from the source of a sound would affect response time?

_____

_____

5. The speed of sound in air is 343 meters per second at 20°C. The speed of sound increases as air temperature increases at a rate of 0.6 meters per second for each degree Celsius increase. Do you think an increase in air temperature would significantly increase your response time in this experiment? Why or why not?

_____

_____

_____

_____

_____

Further Explorations

1. Use this experiment to compare response times between students and teachers.

2. Do the same experiment, but use the LED light on the ultrasonic motion detector as a visual stimulus to start running. Compare visual response time to auditory response time.

Lab 9 Breathing and Heart Rate

Was there ever a time when you were under a condition of high emotional stress and started to breathe rapidly? An excessive increase in breathing rate is called hyperventilation. A decrease in breathing rate is called hypoventilation. In this lab, you will examine how changes in breathing rate can affect a person's heart rate, or the number of times the heart beats per minute.

Objectives

- Use a heart rate monitor to measure your heart rate.
- Determine how changes in your breathing rate affect your heart rate.

Materials

- ❏ LabPro or CBL 2 unit
- ❏ Vernier Exercise Heart Rate Monitor
- ❏ TI graphing calculator
- ❏ link cable
- ❏ stopwatch or clock with second hand
- ❏ chair
- ❏ saline solution
- ❏ colored pencils (2 colors)
- ❏ laboratory apron
- ❏ goggles

Procedure

Part A. Hyperventilation

1. Connect the LabPro or CBL 2 unit to the graphing calculator using a link cable. Connect the receiver module of the exercise heart rate monitor to Channel 1. Turn on the graphing calculator and start the DATAMATE program. Press CLEAR to reset the program.

2. Elastic straps, for securing the transmitter belt, come in two different sizes (small and large). Select the size of elastic strap that best fits the subject being tested. It is important that the strap provides a snug fit of the trans- mitter belt. Wet each of the electrodes (the two grooved rectangular areas on the under- side of the transmitter belt) with 3 drops of saline solution. Secure the transmitter belt against the skin directly over the base of the rib cage. The POLAR logo on the front of the belt should be centered on the chest. Adjust the elastic strap to ensure a tight fit.

3. Set up the calculator and interface for an exercise heart rate monitor.

a. If the calculator displays HEART RT (BPM) in CH 1, proceed directly to Step 4. If it does not, continue with this step to set up your sensor manually.

b. Select SETUP from the main screen.

c. Press ENTER select CH 1.

d. Select HEART RATE from the SELECT SENSOR menu.

e. Select EX HEART RATE from the HEART RATE menu.

f. Select OK to return to the main screen.

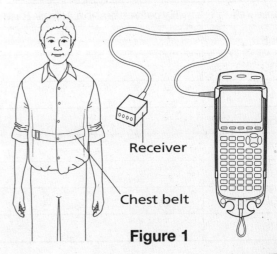

Figure 1

4. Determine that the exercise heart rate monitor is working properly. Heart rate readings displayed on the calculator screen should be steady (±8 beats per minute) and within the normal range of the individual—usually between 60 and 100 beats per minute. If readings appear sporadic, tighten the elastic strap and move the receiver module closer to the center of the transmitter belt. If all equipment is functioning properly, proceed to Step 5.

5. Sit on a chair and breathe at a normal rate. Select START to begin collecting heart rate in beats per minute (BPM). The program displays the average heart rate every 5 seconds on the screen and plots a graph.

6. After collecting data at a normal breathing rate for 60 seconds, continue collecting data while breathing rapidly for the next 30 seconds. **CAUTION:** *If you feel light-headed or dizzy, return to normal breathing immediately.* Breathe normally for another 30 seconds, while continuing to collect data, Then press (STO▶) to stop data collection. A graph of heart rate vs. time will be displayed. Press (▶) to move the trace cursor from one data point to the next. The values of each data point are displayed at the bottom of the calculator screen. Record the data in Table 1. Plot your data from Table 1 on the graph in Data and Observations,

using a colored pencil. Plot time on the x-axis and BPM on the y-axis.

7. Press (ENTER) to return to the main screen.

8. Repeat Part A, steps 2–7, for the other members of your group.

Part B. Hypoventilation

1. Repeat Part A, steps 2–4.

2. After collecting data at a normal breathing rate for 60 seconds, continue collecting data while holding your breath for the next 30 seconds. **CAUTION:** *Take a breath if you need to before the 30 seconds are up.* Breathe normally for another 30 seconds, while continuing to collect data, and then press (STO▶) to stop data collection. A graph of Heart Rate vs. Time will be displayed.

3. Press (▶) to move the trace cursor from one data point to the next. The values of each data point are displayed at the bottom of the calculator screen. Record the data in Table 1. Plot your data from Table 1 on the graph in Data and Observations, using a different colored pencil than the one you used in Part A. Plot time on the x-axis and BPM on the y-axis.

4. Press (ENTER) to return to the main screen.

5. Repeat Part B, steps 1–4, for the other members of your group.

Data and Observations

Table 1

Time (s)	Hyperventilation Heart Rate (BPM)	Hypoventilation Heart Rate (BPM)
15		
30		
45		
60		
75		
90		
105		
120		

Copyright © by Glencoe/McGraw-Hill, a division of the McGraw-Hill Companies, Inc.

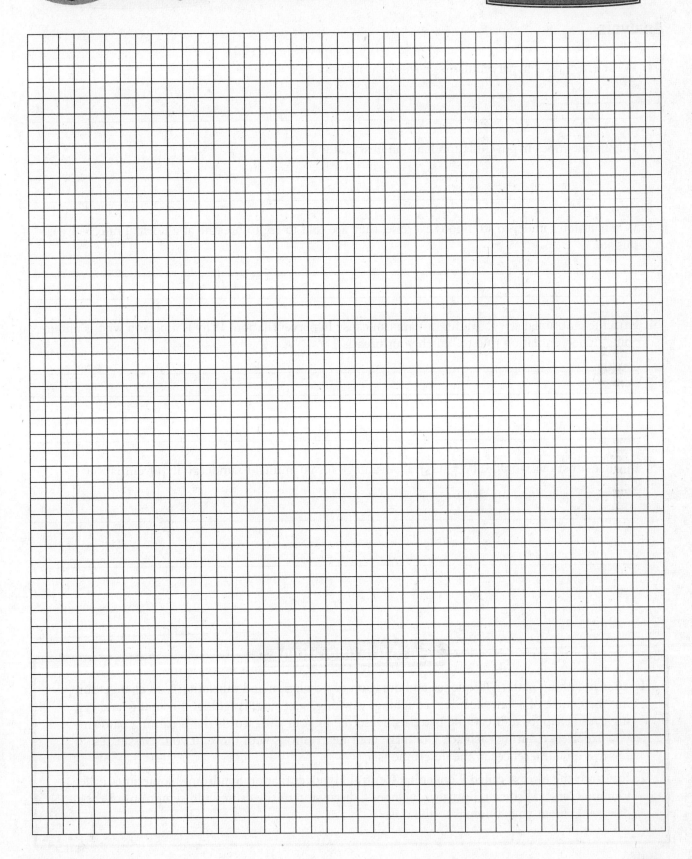

Lab 9 Breathing and Heart Rate, *continued*

Analysis

1. What effect does hyperventilation have on heart rate?

_____

_____

2. What effect does hypoventilation have on heart rate?

_____

_____

3. When athletes undergo strenuous exercise, they are told to try to breathe at a normal rate. Why is this so?

_____

_____

4. Extreme emotional stress, fright, or pain can cause hyperventilation. Why is a person who is undergoing hyperventilation told to "catch your breath"?

_____

_____

_____

_____

5. In what situations would it be a survival advantage for an animal to undergo hypoventilation?

_____

_____

_____

_____

Further Explorations

1. Your breathing pattern (sequence and duration of exhalation and inhalation) can change during the course of a day. Sleeping, coughing, yawning, sneezing, laughing, hiccuping, and crying cause changes in breathing patterns. Describe in your own words the breathing pattern you experience during each act. Compare your descriptions with those of your classmates. Discuss any differences in the descriptions.

2. Research the disease called Congenital Central Hypoventilation Syndrome, sometimes called Ondine Curse. Write a report that includes a discussion of the causes and symptoms of the disease. Present your findings to the class.

Lab 10 — What is the effect of exercise on heart rate?

The heart pumps blood to all the cells of the body. As a person exercises, the muscle cells use increased amounts of oxygen and food, which must be replaced by the blood. The muscle cells also produce more wastes, which must be removed by the blood. In this lab, you will design an experiment to test the effects of exercise and other factors on a person's heart rate, which is the number of heartbeats per minute. You will use a heart rate monitor to measure heart rate.

Problem

Does a shift in body position cause a person's heart rate to change? How does exercise affect heart rate? After exercising, how long does it take for a person's heart to recover, that is, return to its resting rate?

Hypothesis

Write a hypothesis about how exercise and body position affect a person's heart rate.

_____

_____

Objectives

- Hypothesize about the effects of body position and exercise on heart rate.
- Use a heart rate monitor to measure heart rate.
- Compare the effects of different body positions and exercises on heart rate.
- After performing different exercises, determine the heart's recovery time.

Possible Materials

- ❏ LabPro or CBL 2 unit
- ❏ TI graphing calculator
- ❏ link cable
- ❏ Vernier Exercise Heart Rate Monitor
- ❏ stopwatch or clock with second hand
- ❏ saline solution
- ❏ exercise equipment
- ❏ laboratory apron
- ❏ goggles

Lab 10 What is the effect of exercise on heart rate?, *continued*

Plan the Experiment

1. Devise a procedure that tests the effects of body position and various exercises on heart rate, and determines the heart's recovery time after each exercise. The procedure should include a probeware system consisting of an exercise heart rate monitor, LabPro or CBL 2 interface, TI graphing calculator, and link cable.

2. Choose body positions and exercises that are safe for you. **CAUTION:** *If you have any medical conditions that may be aggravated by these movements, inform your teacher.* In your procedure, include how long you will maintain each body position and perform each exercise, as well as how many measurements you will make. Think about what your control will be in the experiment.

3. Connect the LabPro or CBL 2 unit to the graphing calculator using a link cable. Connect the receiver module of the exercise heart rate monitor to CH 1. Turn on the graphing calculator and start the DATAMATE program. Press CLEAR to reset the program.

4. Elastic straps, for securing the transmitter belt, come in two different sizes (small and large). Select the size of elastic strap that best fits the subject being tested. It is important that the strap provides a snug fit of the transmitter belt. Wet each of the electrodes (the two grooved rectangular areas on the underside of the transmitter belt) with 3 drops of saline solution. Secure the transmitter belt against the skin directly over the base of the rib cage. The POLAR logo on the front of the belt should be centered on the chest. Adjust the elastic strap to ensure a tight fit.

5. Set up the calculator and interface for an Exercise Heart Rate Monitor.

   a. If the calculator displays HEART RT (BPM) in CH 1, proceed directly to Step 6. If it does not, continue with this step to set up your sensor manually.

   b. Select SETUP from the main screen.

   c. Press ENTER select CH 1.

   d. Select HEART RATE from the SELECT SENSOR menu.

e. Select EX HEART RATE from the HEART RATE menu.

f. Select OK to return to the main screen.

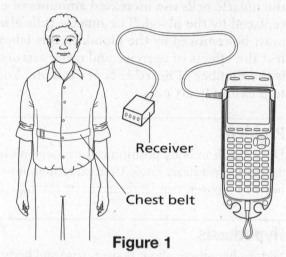

Figure 1

Receiver

Chest belt

6. Determine that the exercise heart rate monitor is working properly. Heart rate readings displayed on the calculator screen should be steady (± 8 beats per minute) and within the normal range of the individual—usually between 60 and 100 beats per minute. If readings appear sporadic, tighten the elastic strap and move the receiver module closer to the center of the transmitter belt. If all equipment is functioning properly, proceed to Step a.

   a. Plan each trial. Trials should include measuring the average resting heart rate for several different body positions.

   b. For exercise trials, be sure to continue collecting data until the resting heart rate is reached. Recovery time is the amount of time it takes to reach the resting heart rate after exercise has stopped.

   c. Select START to begin collecting heart rate in beats per minute (BPM). The program displays the average heart rate every 5 seconds on the screen and plots a graph.

   d. Start the exercise to be tested. A graph of heart rate vs. time will be plotted while the exercise is being performed.

   e. When you are finished exercising, wait until the resting heart rate is reached and press STO to stop data collection.

What is the effect of exercise on heart rate?, *continued*

A scaled graph of heart rate vs. time will be displayed. Press [▶] to move the trace cursor from one data point to the next. The values of each data point are displayed at the bottom of the calculator screen. Record the data in Tables 1 and 2.

f. Press [ENTER] to return to the main screen.

g. Repeat steps c–f for each heart rate trial.

7. Use Tables 1 and 2 to record your data, or you may wish to make your own data tables.

8. Write your procedure on another sheet of paper or in your notebook. It should include any types of exercise equipment you use.

Check the Plan

1. Your experiment should include a control.

2. Be sure that the exercises you do are not time-consuming and cause little disruption to other groups in the classroom.

3. Choose exercises that are safe.

4. Make sure your teacher has approved your experimental plan before you proceed further.

5. Carry out the experiment.

Data and Observations

Table 1

Body Position	Average Resting Heart Rate (BPM)

Table 2

Effect of Exercise on Heart Rate			
Type of exercise	Duration of exercise (minutes)	Maximum heart rate during exercise (BPM)	Recovery time (seconds)

Lab 10   What is the effect of exercise on heart rate?, *continued*

Analysis

1. What was the control in your experiment? What did it show?

_____

_____

2. What body position resulted in the highest heart rate? Explain why.

_____

_____

3. What type of exercise increased your heart rate the most? The least?

_____

_____

4. Explain why the exercises you identified in your answer to question 3 had different effects on heart rate.

_____

_____

5. What is the relationship between type of exercise, heart rate, and recovery time?

_____

_____

6. Two people who have performed the same exercise for the same amount of time may show different recovery times. Why do you think this is so?

_____

_____

_____

7. What factors, other than exercise and body position, may affect heart rate?

_____

_____

Checking Your Hypothesis

Was your hypothesis supported by your data? Why or why not?

_____

_____

Further Investigations

1. Pool class data to compare the average heart rate of males with that of females in your class.

2. Use the probeware system you used in the lab to observe the effects of different factors on heart rate. You might consider testing the effects of time of day, type or amount of food consumed, or stress.

Appendix

Dissolved Oxygen Concentrations

Use this table to calibrate the dissolved oxygen probe used in Lab 3 *Testing Water Quality*.

Dissolved Oxygen (mg/L) in Air-Saturated Distilled Water								
	Barometric Pressure							
Air Temperature	770 mm Hg	760 mm Hg	750 mm Hg	740 mm Hg	730 mm Hg	720 mm Hg	710 mm Hg	700 mm Hg
17°C	9.86	9.74	9.61	9.48	9.35	9.22	9.10	8.97
18°C	9.67	9.54	9.41	9.29	9.16	9.04	8.91	8.79
19°C	9.47	9.35	9.23	9.11	8.98	8.86	8.74	8.61
20°C	9.29	9.17	9.05	8.93	8.81	8.69	8.57	8.45
21°C	9.11	9.00	8.88	8.76	8.64	8.52	8.40	8.28
22°C	8.94	8.83	8.71	8.59	8.48	8.36	8.25	8.13
23°C	8.78	8.66	8.55	8.44	8.32	8.21	8.09	7.98
24°C	8.62	8.51	8.40	8.28	8.17	8.06	7.95	7.84
25°C	8.47	8.36	8.25	8.14	8.03	7.92	7.81	7.70
26°C	8.32	8.21	8.10	7.99	7.89	7.78	7.67	7.56
27°C	8.17	8.07	7.96	7.86	7.75	7.64	7.54	7.43

Lab 1

Is oxygen cycled in the environment?

Objectives

- Hypothesize whether oxygen is cycled between plants and animals in the environment.
- Design a closed aquatic system that does not allow gases to enter or leave.
- Interpret data to determine whether oxygen is cycled between plants and animals.

Process Skills

form hypotheses, experiment, interpret data

Time Allotment

2 class periods

Possible Hypotheses

Students may hypothesize that because plants give off oxygen and animals need oxygen to live, animals take in the oxygen that plants produce.

Possible Materials

LabPro or CBL 2 interfaces (6)
TI graphing calculator (6)
AC adapter (optional) (6)
link cables (6)
Vernier dissolved oxygen probes (6)
small, clear containers with caps (1 for each closed system)
aquatic animal, such as a snail (1 for each closed system containing an animal)
aquatic plant, such as *Elodea* (1 for each closed system containing a plant)
tap water (allowed to stand for one day)
artificial light source
D.O. electrode filling solution (KCl solution) (6 bottles, included with the probes)

Beral pipettes (6)
metric rulers (6)
100-mL graduated cylinders (6)
10-mL graduated cylinders (6)
250-mL beakers (1 for each closed system)
distilled water (600 mL)
wax marking pencils (6)
lab wipes (1 package)
laboratory aprons (30)
goggles (30)

Possible Procedures

Students might set up sealed test tubes as listed in Table 1 on the next page.

Teaching the Lab

Have students work in groups of five.

- Check the number of days students are waiting before testing the dissolved oxygen levels. A reasonable time is 3 to 5 days. If students wait too long, the animals might die.
- Avoid placing the closed systems close to an incandescent light. The heat may harm the organisms. A fluorescent or growth lightbulb will work well.
- The dissolved oxygen probe can be stored for several days with filling solution inside, as long as the membrane tip is submerged in water.
- The lab procedure does not require students to perform a new calibration for the dissolved oxygen probe. The stored calibration will work well when comparing a change in dissolved oxygen concentration in sealed samples. If you wish your students to perform a new calibration, refer to the probe booklet that came with the dissolved oxygen probe.

Data and Observations

Sample data below were obtained using *Elodea* and snails that were exposed to light for three days.

Copyright © by Glencoe/McGraw-Hill, a division of the McGraw-Hill Companies, Inc.

Table 1 Sample data after 3-day light exposure

Descriptions of Closed Systems	Concentration of Dissolved Oxygen (ppm)
Water only (control)	7.8
Elodea in water	12.2
Snail in water	4.9
Snail and *Elodea* in water	11.1

Analysis

1. Students should observe that the closed aquatic system containing only water and the plant had the highest concentration of dissolved oxygen. Photosynthesis caused the high oxygen level.

2. Students should observe that the closed aquatic system containing only water and the animal had the lowest concentration of dissolved oxygen. The animal took in some of the oxygen that had been dissolved in the water.

3. Students should observe that the system containing the plant and animal has an oxygen concentration lower than that of the system containing only the plant but higher than the system containing only the animal. The animal took some of the oxygen produced by the plant.

4. An open system would have allowed oxygen from outside the container to dissolve in the water, thereby interfering with the results.

Checking Your Hypothesis

Answers will vary. If students said that, because plants give off the oxygen animals need to live, it is likely that oxygen cycles between them, then the data should support their hypothesis.

Lab 2
An Environmental Limiting Factor

Objectives
- Use a pH sensor to measure pH.
- Measure and compare the pH of soil and water samples.
- Evaluate the pH of the samples as an environmental limiting factor.

Process Skills
observe, communicate, measure, interpret data

Time Allotment
one-half class period to prepare soil and water samples; one class period to measure pH of samples and record data

Materials
LabPro or CBL 2 units (6)
TI graphing calculators (6)
link cables (6)
pH sensors (6)
250-mL beakers (12)
soil samples (18 or more)
plastic bags (18 or more)
large spoons (6)
distilled water (1-gallon bottle)
water samples from various bodies of water (6)
water samples from precipitation (6)
water samples from the ocean or a saltwater aquarium (6)
samples of drinking water (6)
paper plates (18)
mortars and pestles (6 of each)
balances (6)
jars with lids (48)
wax marking pencils (6)
plastic or rubber gloves (30 pairs)
laboratory aprons (30)
goggles (30)

Preparation
- Soil samples need to be collected several days in advance. Allow time during class for collection, or supply students with clean jars and ask them to bring samples from various sources to class.
- Watch for a rainy or snowy day to collect precipitation water samples.
- pH Sensor Calibration: For greater accuracy, you may have students calibrate the pH sensor before use. If so, prepare or purchase the buffer solutions in advance. Vernier Software and other science suppliers sell a package for preparing buffer solutions. Sensor calibration could be done the day before the lab or on the day of the lab. A pH 4.0 and pH 10.0 buffer solution is desirable. Place the pH sensor into the buffer solution and carefully swirl the solution so the electrode makes good contact. Select SETUP from the main menu. Select CALIBRATE from the SETUP menu. Select CALIBRATE NOW and follow the on-screen instructions to calibrate the pH sensor.

Teaching the Lab
Have students work in groups of five.
- Remind students to rinse the pH sensor tip before each use and to keep the tip moist.

Data and Observations
Student data on water and soil samples will vary.

Analysis
1. Students' answers will vary. Garden soils where azaleas, hydrangea, or rhododendrons are grown may be acidic. The pH of saltwater aquarium water is about 8. Distilled water should be pH 7. Tap water may vary above pH 7. In the eastern United States and Canada, precipitation may be as low as pH 4.
2. Students' answers will vary. Some plants may be able to grow in soils with a range of pH values, while others may be found only in soils of a certain acidity.

3. If the ground provides natural buffering, the bodies of water may have a higher pH than precipitation.

4. Students' answers will vary. Some municipal water supplies adjust the pH of drinking water.

5. Students' answers will vary. However, the water source with the greatest acidity should be identified as the greatest limiting factor.

Lab 3
Testing Water Quality

Objectives

- Using a dissolved oxygen probe, measure the concentration of dissolved oxygen in water samples obtained from various locations.
- Give reasons why the water samples have different concentrations of dissolved oxygen.

Process Skills

observe, measure, predict, infer

Time Allotment

time outside of class to collect water samples; 1 class period to conduct the lab

Materials

LabPro or CBL 2 units (6)

AC adapters (optional) (6)

TI graphing calculators (6)

link cables (6)

Vernier dissolved oxygen probes (6)

sodium sulfite calibration solution (6 bottles, included with the probes)

D.O. electrode filling solution (KCl solution) (6 bottles, included with the probes)

Beral pipettes (6)

dissolved oxygen calibration bottles (6, included with the probes)

classroom thermometer

classroom barometer

metric rulers (6)

water samples from different locations (at least 4 samples for each group)

jars with lids (24 or more)

plastic or rubber gloves (30 pairs)

100-mL graduated cylinders (6)

10-mL graduated cylinders (6)

250-mL beakers (30)

distilled water (600 mL)

wax marking pencils (6)

lab wipes (1 package)

laboratory aprons (30)

goggles (30)

Preparation

- To make more sodium sulfite solution, see page T10.

Teaching the Lab

Have students work in groups of five.

- When students are finished with the sodium sulfite solution, they should gently squeeze the bottle before closing it to remove air from the top of the bottle.

- Discuss with students the concepts behind the calibration procedure. Sodium sulfite removes dissolved oxygen from a solution. If the sodium sulfite solution has been stored brim full in its bottle, you can assume it is oxygen-free. A second calibration point is the value of dissolved oxygen in air-saturated distilled water. These two points can set up a calibration line with a defined slope.

- The dissolved oxygen probe can be stored for several days with filling solution inside, as long as the membrane tip is submerged in water. If the probe is stored longer, the inside of the membrane cap must be rinsed and dried prior to storage.

Data and Observations

Table 1 Sample observations and data

Sample	Water Source	Observations of Water	Concentration of Dissolved Oxygen (ppm)
1	Tap	Clear	7.62
2	Aquarium	No water movement; stagnant	7.12
3	River	Murky; somewhat polluted	4.12
4	Puddle with algae	Green-colored	11.60

Analysis

1. Answers will vary. Water that is flowing, being bubbled with air, or populated with photosynthetic organisms will have a high dissolved-oxygen concentration. Stagnant, polluted, or very warm water will have low dissolved-oxygen concentrations.

2. **a.** Samples with a dissolved oxygen concentration lower than 4 ppm could not support aquatic life.

   b. Aquatic organisms are unable to get the oxygen they need from the air. The oxygen must be dissolved in the water in which they live.

3. Dissolved oxygen in water comes primarily from aquatic organisms undergoing photosynthesis. The deeper the water, the less light is available for photosynthesis. Therefore, the concentration of dissolved oxygen decreases with water depth.

4. Students might say they did not warm up or calibrate the probe properly, did not swirl the samples with the probe, or had introduced air into the samples by shaking them.

Lab 4

How well does yeast ferment different sugars?

Objectives

- Hypothesize whether yeast ferments some sugars betters than others.
- Using a carbon dioxide gas sensor, measure the amount of carbon dioxide gas produced by the fermentation of different sugars by yeast.
- Compare how well yeast ferments different sugars.

Process Skills

form hypotheses, use numbers, experiment, separate and control variables, interpret data

Time Allotment

1 class period to design the lab; 1 class period to conduct the lab

Possible Hypotheses

Students may say that yeast ferments different sugars equally well or that yeast is able to ferment some sugars better than others.

Possible Materials

LabPro or CBL 2 units (6)

carbon dioxide sensors (6)

TI graphing calculators (6)

link cables (6)

AC adaptors (6)

different kinds of sugar solutions, such as glucose, sucrose, fructose, dextrose, maltose, lactose (12 mL of each)

yeast suspension (12 mL per 12 mL sugar solutions made)

test tubes (6)

stirring rods (6)

10-mL graduated cylinders (6)

thermometers (6)

water baths (6)

hot and cold water

containers for fermentation chambers (6)

clock or watches with second hand (6)

thermal mitts (8 pairs)

laboratory aprons (30)

goggles (30)

Possible Procedures

- Students might make a fermentation mixture by combining 2 mL yeast suspension with 2 mL sugar solution and allowing the mixture to incubate for 10 minutes at 37°C before placing 1 mL of the mixture in the fermentation chamber.
- The fermentation chamber should fit the carbon dioxide sensor. The following containers might be used as a fermentation chamber: test tube, culture flask, 20-oz (591-mL) plastic bottle.

Preparation

- To make the yeast suspension, see page T10.
- 5% sugar solutions can be used. See page T10 for directions.

Teaching the Lab

Have students work in groups of five.

- If students are unable to print their graphs from their graphing calculators, they can plot the graphs on graph paper.

Data and Observations

Students may record in Table 1 that bubbles formed to varying degrees in the fermentation chambers.

Table 2 Sample data

Carbon Dioxide Concentration (ppm)					
Time (seconds)	Sugar used: None	Sugar used: Glucose	Sugar used: Sucrose	Sugar used: Fructose	Sugar used: Lactose
30	989	1715	1752	1763	1269
60	987	2063	2110	1968	1298
90	989	2554	2499	2399	1320
120	995	3125	3210	2690	1365
150	998	3714	3745	3268	1420
180	1002	4169	4230	3502	1490
210	1001	4580	4550	3987	1520
240	1002	4889	4966	4102	1556

Analysis

1. The fermentation rates (ppm/s) from the sample data are: control, 0.0806; glucose, 15.9671; sucrose, 16.0421; fructose, 12.0456; lactose, 1.46191.

2. Using the sample data, glucose and sucrose were fermented the best by the yeast. Lactose was not fermented very well.

3. Students might say that yeast ferments some sugars better than others because the yeast can transport those sugars into the cell more easily or has the enzymes needed to ferment those sugars at a faster rate.

4. The yeast enzymes that are involved in fermentation function best at 37°C.

5. Students might say that they kept constant the amount of yeast used, the amount of sugar used, the temperature at which fermentation took place, and the type of chamber in which fermentation took place.

6. The carbon dioxide concentration in the control chamber was due to the presence of carbon dioxide in the air within the chamber.

Checking Your Hypothesis

Answers will vary. Students who hypothesized that yeast ferments some sugars better than others will say that their hypothesis was supported by the data.

Lab 5

How can pH be used to compare rates of photosynthesis?

Objectives

- Make a hypothesis about the effect of light intensity on the rate of photosynthesis.

- Expose an aquatic plant to different intensities of light.

- Use a probe to measure the pH of water samples.

- Compare the rates of photosynthesis of an aquatic plant exposed to different light intensities.

Process Skills

form hypotheses, measure, experiment, separate and control variables, interpret data

Time Allotment

1 class period to set up the lab; 15 minutes per class period as needed to measure pH

Possible Hypotheses

Students may hypothesize that increased light intensity increases the rate of photosynthesis or has no effect on the rate of photosynthesis. Students probably will not hypothesize that decreasing light intensity increases the rate of photosynthesis, as they know that light is needed for photosynthesis to occur.

Possible Materials

LabPro or CBL 2 units (6)

TI graphing calculators (6)

link cables (6)

AC adapters (optional) (6)

pH sensors (6)

aquatic plant, such as *Elodea* (at least 12 of the same kind)

large test tubes with stoppers (24 or more)

test-tube racks (6)

various light sources

dechlorinated water (1200 mL)

rinse bottles of distilled water (6)

250-mL beakers (6)

laboratory aprons (30)

goggles (30)

Possible Procedures

Students may decide to set up one test tube of water with an *Elodea* sprig exposed to room light, one test tube of water with an *Elodea* sprig exposed to bright light from a lamp, and one test tube of water with an *Elodea* sprig exposed to darkness. The test tubes should be stoppered. As a control, students should test the pH of the water before beginning the experiment.

Teaching the Lab

Have students work in groups of five.

- To more readily observe increases in the pH of the water due to photosynthesis, have students use a straw to blow carbon dioxide into the dechlorinated water before beginning the experiment. This will decrease the initial pH of the water.

Data and Observations

Table 1 Sample data obtained from *Elodea* sprigs

	pH of Samples		
Day	Type of light intensity: **Darkness**	Type of light intensity: **Average room light**	Type of light intensity: **Bright light**
0	6.4	6.4	6.4
1	5.9	6.7	7.1

Analysis

1. Answers may include test-tube size, the amount of water in the test tubes, the type of plant used, plant size, and the initial pH of the water.

2. Students should find that the sample exposed to the highest light intensity had the highest pH, whereas the sample exposed to the lowest light intensity had the lowest pH.

3. The sample exposed to the highest light intensity had the highest pH because it used up much of the carbon dioxide from the water due to a high rate of photosynthesis. The decrease in the carbon dioxide level caused a marked decrease in the level of carbonic acid, resulting in a high pH. The opposite is true for the sample exposed to the lowest light intensity. If students exposed a sample to darkness, the sample probably showed a pH level that was lower than that of the initial pH of the water because the plant did not photosynthesize but did respire. During respiration, the plant released carbon dioxide into the water, which increased the level of carbonic acid and lowered the pH.

4. Outdoor plants would be expected to undergo the highest rate of photosynthesis around noon, when the sun is directly overhead and the sunlight reaching the plants is most intense.

5. Most photosynthetic organisms are found near the surface of the ocean because sunlight is most intense there, allowing the organisms to undergo a higher rate of photosynthesis.

Checking Your Hypothesis

Answers will vary. Students who hypothesized that increased light intensity increases the rate of photosynthesis will say that their hypothesis was supported by the data.

Lab 6

Effect of Environmental Temperature on the Metabolic Rates of Animals

Objectives

- Use a carbon dioxide gas sensor to measure carbon dioxide concentrations.
- Determine the metabolic rate of small animals by measuring their rate of carbon dioxide production.
- Explain the effect of temperature on the metabolic rate of cold-blooded animals.

Process Skills

measure, use numbers, experiment, communicate, interpret data

Time Allotment

1 class period

Materials

LabPro or CBL 2 units (6)

TI graphing calculators (6)

link cables (6)

carbon dioxide sensors (6)

250-mL respiration chambers (6) (come with probes)

thermometers (6)

crickets or pill bugs (24–60)

ice (one bag or several trays)

warm tap water

500-mL or 1000-mL beakers (6)

balances (6)

Beral pipettes or small beakers (6)

paper towels (1 roll or 30 pieces)

laboratory aprons (30)

goggles (30)

Preparation

- Crickets can be purchased from a pet store or a biological supply house. Pill bugs can be easily maintained in a terrarium with some sticks, leaf matter, and an occasional piece of fruit.
- The stored values of calibration information in the DATAMATE program for the carbon dioxide probe should work fine for this lab.

Teaching the Lab

Have students work in groups of five.

- Students should keep the animals being tested in the temperature range 10–35°C so the animals are not stressed.
- Remind students to keep the carbon dioxide probe away from water, which may damage it.

Data and Observations

Animal Type <u>Crickets</u>

Table 1 Sample Data

Group	Animal Mass (g)	Temperature (°C)	CO_2 Production Rate (ppm/s)	CO_2 Production Rate per Gram (ppm/s·g)
1	3.1	4	0.297	0.096
2	3.1	11.2	0.812	0.26
3	3.1	15	1.527	0.49
4	3.1	31.5	3.900	1.3
5	3.1	38	5.327	1.7

Analysis

1. Answers appear in Table 1. Answers will vary depending on animal mass and CO_2 concentration values.

2. See sample graph. (There will only be three data points on the graph.)

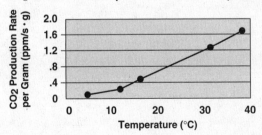

CO_2 Production Rate per Gram versus Temperature

3. Student answers may vary depending on results. Students should find that the carbon dioxide production rate increases as the temperature rises. The lowest rate should be at 10°C and the highest rate at 35°C.

4. Student answers may vary depending on individual results. As temperature increases, the metabolic rate increases, as indicated by the increase in carbon dioxide production. Within the temperature limits for the animals, the increase is usually exponential. It is common for the metabolic rate near 40°C to be 8 times that at 10°C.

5. The ability to change skin color can help lizards control their internal body temperature, which will affect their rate of metabolic activity. A change to a dark color is advantageous when the lizard is cold, since dark skin will absorb radiant heat, allowing the lizard to be more active. A change to a lighter skin color when the lizard is warm will allow it to reflect radiant heat, keeping itself from overheating.

Lab 7

What is the effect of exercise on body temperature?

Objectives

- Hypothesize about the effect of exercise on body surface temperature.
- Measure body surface temperature using a temperature probe.
- Compare body surface temperature while at rest with body surface temperature while exercising.

Process Skills

form hypotheses, measure, experiment, separate and control variables, interpret data

Time Allotment

1 class period

Possible Hypotheses

Hypotheses may vary. Students may say that body surface temperature will increase with exercise or that the temperature will decrease, due to sweating.

Possible Materials

LabPro or CBL 2 units (6)

TI graphing calculators (6)

link cables (6)

temperature probes or surface temperature sensors (6)

athletic tape (1 roll)

material for insulating the temperature probes, such as wool or polyester fill (2 × 2-inch piece for each probe)

plastic bags to cover the temperature probes (6)

laboratory aprons (30)

goggles (30)

Possible Procedures

Students may decide to measure an individual's body surface temperature on the forehead, inside the elbow, or on a calf muscle. Students might run, climb stairs, or work out on an exercise machine. The LabPro or CBL 2 unit and graphing calculator can be held by an individual while exercising.

Teaching the Lab

Have students work in groups of five.

- Do not allow students to exercise if they have a history of exercise-induced asthma, heart disorder, or any other condition that may be aggravated by exercise.
- Check students' procedures before they do the experiment. Make sure that their experiment includes a control.

Data and Observations

Table 1 Sample data

Resting Temperatures	
Body location	Temperature (C°)
Forehead	34.2
Underarm	34.4
Calf	32.5
Between thumb and fingers	33.7
Ankle	32.3
Inner side of elbow	34.9

Table 2 Sample data

Exercise Temperatures	
Body location: inner side of elbow Type of exercise: running	
Time (seconds)	Temperature °(C)
0	34.9
20	35.5
40	35.6
60	35.8
80	35.8
100	35.9
120	35.9
140	35.8
160	35.9
180	35.8
200	35.9

Analysis

1. The control was the surface temperature of the chosen body location before exercising. The control showed that any subsequent change in temperature was due to exercise.

2. Answers will vary. Students might say that body locations that are less exposed to the air or have fewer sweat glands have a higher surface temperature.

3. Students' data should show that exercise increases body surface temperature. That is because muscles produce heat when they contract.

4. Students' data should show an initial increase in body surface temperature followed by a leveling off of temperature. The temperature does not continue to increase because of the body's cooling mechanisms.

5. Wearing insulating clothing while exercising would probably result in a higher body surface temperature because the clothing would keep the radiated heat near the surface of the body.

Checking Your Hypothesis

Answers will vary. Students who hypothesized that exercise increases body surface temperature will say that their hypothesis was supported by the data.

Lab 8
Measuring Response Time

Objectives

- Use a motion detector to determine the time it takes for a person to respond after hearing a sound.
- Conduct repeated trials and calculate an average response time.
- Compare the response times of different individuals.

Process Skills

observe, recognize and use spatial relationships, measure, use numbers, interpret data

Time Allotment

1 class period

Materials

C-clamps (provided with newer model
 motion detectors) (6)

LabPro or CBL 2 units (6)

TI graphing calculators (6)

link cables (6)

motion detectors (6)

Preparation

- Use an area as free of objects as possible. Stationary chairs, tables, and other objects in the beam of the motion detector can produce unwanted echoes and cause problems with the data collection. If you cannot move these objects, try placing a cloth over them to minimize sound reflection.

- The floor underneath the motion detector can also cause unwanted sound reflections. If this is a problem, aim the motion detector slightly upward. If the problem persists, try placing a cloth horizontally just in front of and below the motion detector.

- Placing the motion detector about 4 meters from a wall gives a good reference line on the graph. See the horizontal line in the sample graph in Figure 1.

- The minimum range of the motion detector is about 0.5 meters, while the maximum range is 6 meters. A distance of 4 meters from the wall produces few echoes and therefore gives good readings.

Teaching the Lab

- Remind students not to use visual clues to start their response motion. They are testing their response to an auditory stimulus.

- If students are not getting good graphs of their data, try adjusting the time graph settings under the SETUP menu. Sometimes the motion detector works better at one rate than another.

- It is sometimes helpful for the runner to hold a large, flat object (a large book or a pizza box) to reflect the sound waves toward the motion detector. Irregular reflecting surfaces sometimes cause the reflected sound waves to bounce erratically.

Data and Observations

Table 1 Sample data

	Response Time (seconds)				
Trial	Student #1 Age:	Student #2 Age:	Student #3 Age:	Student #4 Age:	Student #5 Age:
1	1.07899	1.59251	1.19875	1.29540	1.39875
2	1.05847	1.69873	1.17962	1.27697	1.35789
3	1.06983	1.75874	1.21698	1.21147	1.36987
4	1.04590	1.48999	1.19144	1.20587	1.32010
5	1.03698	1.43690	1.18364	1.19581	1.28975
Average	1.05803	1.59537	1.19355	1.23710	1.34727

Analysis

1. Answers will vary. Student should choose the lowest time from all the trials.

2. Answers will vary. Some students' response times might drop as more trials are done. They might say that they could learn to respond faster as they got more practice with the experimental procedure.

3. Answers will vary. Students might see some differences between ages, but the difference may not be large.

4. Students may guess that sounds that come from a greater distance would take longer to reach a person's ears, so that extra time would have to be added into the response time.

5. Answers will vary. Students might say that a small change in temperature would not increase the speed of sound enough to change response times significantly.

Lab 9
Breathing and Heart Rate

Objectives
- Use a heart rate monitor to measure your heart rate.
- Determine how changes in your breathing rate affect your heart rate.

Process Skills
measure, use numbers, interpret data

Time Allotment
1 class period

Materials
LabPro or CBL 2 units (6)

Vernier Exercise Heart Rate Monitors (6)

TI graphing calculators (6)

link cables (6)

stopwatches or clock with second hand (6)

chairs (6)

saline solution

colored pencils (6 each of 2 colors)

laboratory aprons (30)

goggles (30)

Preparation
- Make sure you have enough chairs for students to sit on.

Teaching the Lab
Have students work in groups of five.

- Tell students to be patient when using the heart rate monitor.
- Warn students that while hyperventilating during Part A, they could become dizzy and could lose their balance. For that reason, students must remain seated during this lab.

- After students complete the lab, you might wish to explain that increased breathing causes more carbon dioxide to be expelled from the body than usual. This upsets the carbonic acid/hydrogen carbonate ion buffering system in the blood, which acts to maintain a constant blood pH. As more carbon dioxide is expelled, the blood's pH rises. The body responds to the increased pH level by constricting blood vessels, thereby causing the heart rate to increase. The constriction of blood vessels in the brain causes the person to become dizzy and eventually lose consciousness. At that point, the body's reflex mechanisms usually restore normal breathing. As a result, blood pH returns to normal.

Data and Observations
Sample data from parts A and B are shown in the table below. Students' graphs will vary, depending on the data they collected. Time, in seconds, should be plotted on the x-axis, and heart rate, in BPM, should be plotted on the y-axis. The graphs should show a peak during hyperventilation and a dip during hypoventilation.

Table 1 Sample data

Time (s)	Hyperventilation Heart Rate (BPM)	Hypoventilation Heart Rate (BPM)
15	70	71
30	72	70
45	71	70
60	76	68
75	84	65
90	81	67
105	74	70
120	72	72

Analysis
1. Hyperventilation increases heart rate.
2. Hypoventilation decreases heart rate.
3. Students might say that strenuous exercise could cause athletes to breathe rapidly, leading to dizziness and light-headedness. Breathing at a normal rate will help prevent these problems.
4. Students might say that "catching your breath" is just a way of trying to breathe at a

normal rate compared to the rapid breathing that occurs when a person is frightened or under stress.

5. Answers will vary. Hypoventilation is an advantage for animals that dive underwater for long periods of time. Holding their breath causes the animals' heart rate to decrease. When the heart rate decreases, so does the amount of carbon dioxide that builds up in the blood. Hypoventilation is also an advantage for animals that hibernate.

Lab 10

What is the effect of exercise on heart rate?

Objectives

- Hypothesize about the effects of body position and exercise on heart rate.
- Use a heart rate monitor to measure heart rate.
- Compare the effects of different body positions and exercises on heart rate.
- After performing different exercises, determine the heart's recovery time.

Process Skills

form hypotheses, measure, experiment, separate and control variables, interpret data

Time Allotment

1 class period to design the lab; 1 class period to conduct the lab

Possible Hypotheses

Students may hypothesize that exercises and body positions that require increased use of muscles will increase heart rate.

Possible Materials

LabPro or CBL 2 units (60)

TI graphing calculators (6)

link cables (6)

exercise equipment

Vernier Exercise Heart Rate Monitors (6)

saline solution

stopwatches or clock with second hand (6)

laboratory aprons (30)

goggles (30)

Possible Procedures

Types of possible exercises that can be used for this Investigation include climbing stairs, jogging, running in place, walking, and jumping rope. Types of possible body positions include reclining, sitting, standing, and bending.

Teaching the Lab

Have students work in groups of five.

- Check students' procedures before they do the experiment.
- Do not allow students to exercise if they have a history of exercise-induced asthma, heart disorder, or any other condition that may be aggravated by exercise.

Data and Observations

Table 1 Sample data

Body Position	Average Resting Heart Rate (BPM)
Reclining	61
Sitting	63
Standing	65

Table 2 Sample data

	Effect of Exercise on Heart Rate		
Type of exercise	Duration of exercise (minutes)	Maximum heart rate during exercise (BPM)	Recovery time (seconds)
None (control)	—	66	—
Jumping rope	10	135	95
Stationary bicycle	10	132	85
Fast walking	10	108	65

Analysis

1. The control should be the heart rate when the muscles are at rest, such as when reclining. The control shows that any changes in the heart rate are due to exercise or a change in body position.

2. Students will probably say that body positions such as standing or bending, which require some exertion, result in the highest heart rate because maintaining those positions requires greater use of muscles.

3. In general, the more strenuous the exercise, the greater is the increase in heart rate.

4. More strenuous exercises require the muscles to work harder, which requires the heart to pump more blood to the muscles.

5. The more strenuous the exercise is, the higher the heart rate, and the greater the recovery time.

6. Recovery time depends on a person's state of physical fitness. The more fit the person is, the shorter the heart's recovery time after exercise.

7. Smoking, caffeine, certain medicines, body weight, and age are some factors that affect heart rate.

Checking Your Hypothesis

Answers will vary. Hypotheses stating that exercise and more strenuous body positions increase heart rate will probably be supported by the data.

Appendix
Analyzing Probeware Lab Data Using Computers

The data collected during a *Probeware Lab* can be imported into a computer for further analysis. This allows the students to work with graphing software to perform more advanced functions than are available on a graphing calculator. Students can create different types of graphs and see the effect their treatment of the data has on the appearance of the graph. Students also can use the computer-generated graph to create reports, posters, and other visual presentations of their data.

Data lists and screen shots can be imported to a desktop computer from a graphing calculator with a **TI-GRAPH LINK*** cable. Each cable connects the port on the bottom edge of the graphing calculator to a free serial or USB port on a Windows computer or to the modem or USB port of a Macintosh computer.

There are several software options that are compatible with the TI-GRAPH LINK cable. Texas Instruments, Inc. has several programs that are written specifically for each type of TI graphing calculator. For instance, **TI-GRAPH LINK TI-73*** is used with a TI-73 graphing calculator. This software allows students to import screen images and data from the calculator to use in other word processing, desktop publishing, or page-layout applications. **TI Connect*** software is a newer software package with enhanced capabilities that also can be used to import and export information from the graphing calculator to a desktop or lap-top computer.

Texas Instruments, Inc. has another software program, **TI InterActive!***, that enables students to import Internet data, perform math calculations, and import data and screen shots from the graphing calculator. The program has a built-in word processing function intergreted into a single program.

Vernier Software & Technology has a program called **Graphical Analysis*** that has similar capabilities. This program was written specifically for science classes. It is easier to use than many business-oriented graphing programs and its capabilities have been tailored to fit the requirements for analyzing scientific data.

Importing data lists from the graphing calculator into **TI Interactive!** or **Graphical Analysis** enables the students to perform in depth mathematical analysis of the data. These programs have the capability of challenging students through the college level.

* Refer to the appropriate hardware or software manuals for details about compatibility and capabilities.